Police Background
Characteristics and
Performance

The New York City-Rand Institute

The New York City-Rand Institute is a nonprofit research institution formed primarily to conduct programs of scientific research and study, and provide reports and recommendations relevant to the operations, planning, or administration of the City of New York. The Institute was established in 1969 as a joint venture by the City of New York and The Rand Corporation as a center for the continuing application of scientific and analytic techniques to problems of urban life and local government. Its trustees are appointed jointly by the City and Rand. Its program includes work on health planning, policy, and delivery; drug abuse; housing; fire protection; criminal justice; welfare; economic development; water resources; and other city problems.

Police Background Characteristics and Performance

Bernard Cohen
Queens College, City University of
New York
The New York City-Rand Institute

Jan M. Chaiken
The New York City-Rand Institute

Lexington Books
D.C. Heath and Company
Lexington, Massachusetts
Toronto   London

This study was sponsored by the National Institute of Law Enforcement and Criminal Justice of the Department of Justice under Grant No. NI-71-030-G (authorizing legislation: The Omnibus Crime Control and Safe Streets Act of 1968). Views or conclusions contained in this study should not be interpreted as representing the official opinion or policy of the City of New York, The New York City-Rand Institute, the National Institute of Law Enforcement and Criminal Justice, the Law Enforcement Assistance Administration, or the Department of Justice.

Library of Congress Cataloging in Publication Data

Cohen, Bernard, 1937-
    Police background characteristics and performance.

    A study conducted by the New York City-Rand Institute for the National Institute of Law Enforcement and Criminal Justice.
    Reprint of the 1972 ed. published by the Rand Corporation, Santa Monica, Calif., which was issued as its Rand report R-999-DOJ.
    Includes bibliographical references.
    1. New York (City)—Police. 2. Prediction of occupational success.
I. Chaiken, Jan M., joint author. II. New York City-Rand Institute.
III. National Institute of Law Enforcement and Criminal Justice.
IV. Title. V. Series: Rand Corporation. Rand report R-999-DOJ.
HV8148.N5C66   363.2'09747'1   73-1000
ISBN 0-669-86835-3

Second printing April 1974.

Published simultaneously in Canada.

Printed in the United States of America.

International Standard Book Number: 0-669-86835-3

Library of Congress Catalog Card Number: 73-1000

To Our Wives

Contents

List of Tables

Preface

This study was conducted at The New York City-Rand Institute under a grant from the National Institute of Law Enforcement and Criminal Justice (Grant Award NI-71-030-G). It is part of a continuing research effort aimed at understanding various aspects of police selection, assignment, promotion, and reward policies. We have compared the background characteristics of a large group of officers in the New York City Police Department with available measures of their performance on the job to determine the type of candidate who is likely to display specific patterns of performance. The implications of the findings for the development of improved performance measures and selection procedures are now being explored and will be described at a later date.

Previous police personnel studies have appeared as New York City-Rand Institute reports and have been utilized by the New York City Police Department. The first report in the series was an analysis of how the Police Department handles allegations of police misconduct, including departmental charges, civilian complaints, harassment, and charges characterizable as corruption.[a] Since the publication of this study, New York City Police Commissioner Patrick V. Murphy has made several changes in the Department's procedures related to allegations of misconduct, as part of his overall program to provide local police commanders with greater authority and to reduce the extent of corruption in the Department.

The second report suggested ways to increase minority representation in the Police Department and led to the establishment of a Personnel Reevaluation and Recruitment Section whose function is to assist minority candidates in completing their applications to the Department.[b]

---

[a]Cohen, Bernard, THE POLICE INTERNAL ADMINISTRATION OF JUSTICE IN NEW YORK CITY, The New York City-Rand Institute, R-621-NYC, November 1970.

[b]Hunt, Isaac C., Jr., and Bernard Cohen, MINORITY RECRUITING IN THE NEW YORK CITY POLICE DEPARTMENT, PART I: THE ATTRACTION OF CANDIDATES, PART II: THE RETENTION OF CANDIDATES, The New York City-Rand Institute, R-702-NYC, May 1971.

Acknowledgments

This study could not have been conducted without the complete support and interest of the New York City Police Department. We are particularly indebted to Police Commissioner Patrick V. Murphy, who reviewed and endorsed our proposal to undertake this work and discussed with us the aspects of police selection of concern to him. We are also indebted to First Deputy Commissioner William H.T. Smith and former Assistant Chief Inspector Sydney C. Cooper, who offered their insights, ideas, and criticism during the conceptualization and research design phase of the study. Thanks are also due to George P. McManus, former Chief Inspector of the Department, and Elmer C. Cone, former Chief of Patrol, whose interest in our research made possible the acquisition of sensitive data from the various personnel units in the Department. Most of our data came from the Chief Clerk's Office, and we are grateful for the special assistance provided to us by Chief Clerk Louis L. Stutman, now Deputy Commissioner of Trials. We are also grateful to John O'Brien, Public Safety Director of New Brunswick, New Jersey (formerly Deputy Inspector, N.Y.P.D.), Donald V. Rowan, Edward Kearney, and Albert Higgins, who served as liaison officers to this study for varying periods of time. They answered innumerable queries and assisted in various arrangements.

Thanks also to Harry I. Bronstein, Director of the Department of Personnel of the City of New York, and Solomon Wiener, Director of Examinations, for providing us access to civil service examination scores, the only information we collected that was not maintained by the New York City Police Department.

Many individuals at The New York City-Rand Institute and The Rand Corporation of Santa Monica, California, provided assistance and inputs which improved the quality of the present research, and we express our thanks to them. First, we wish to express our gratitude to our research assistants Toni Edelman, Margaret Hartz, Kathleen Starger, and Katherine Briar, who had the complex task of collecting data. Their diligence and devotion is attested to by the final utility of our data file. Additional assistance was given by Bertha Palau, Valerie Roye, and Robert Zerafa.

During the course of our study, we benefited greatly from the methodological expertise of three consultants, Edgar F. Borgatta, Joel Lefkowitz, and Burton Singer. All the computer programming for this research was carried out very effectively by Joan Held. We owe a special debt of gratitude to Fred C. Iklé, Social Science Department Head, The Rand Corporation, for his encouragement and support of this research project.

Sincere thanks are due to Melany E. Baehr, Director of The Industrial Relations Center, The University of Chicago; Harrison Campbell and John Jennings of The New York City-Rand Institute; and Marvin E. Wolfgang, Chairman, Department of Sociology of the University of Pennsylvania, and past xviii

Director of Research of the National Commission on the Causes and Prevention of Violence, for their careful reviews of this work.

Finally, we are specially indebted and thankful to Marcia Chaiken and Barbara Cohen for their assistance on this research.

Bernard Cohen—Project Director

Jan M. Chaiken

February, 1973

**Police Background
Characteristics and
Performance**

1   Introduction

During the last decade, three Presidential Commissions have determined that a reduction of crime and disorder in the United States requires an upgrading in the quality of police personnel and their training.[1] Although there is common agreement, within police departments as well as outside, on the desirability of improving police personnel, the selection standards that should be used in achieving this goal are a matter of dispute. In part, this is due to the complexity of the police role in modern society. Not only are patrolmen expected to prevent crime and apprehend criminals, but they also engage in a variety of sensitive order-maintenance and service functions, such as settling marital disputes, aiding accident victims, and directing traffic. In addition, there are many specialized and administrative functions to be performed by policemen, and only a small subgroup of recruits in any given year need to be suitable for them in terms of education and personal characteristics.

To select recruits who will properly perform all these varied functions, it is important to know the types of performance that can be expected from candidates of varying background characteristics. We undertook this study of New York City Police Department personnel with the objective of comparing quantifiable, verified information about the background of recruits with hard data about their later performance. For this purpose we selected a year, 1957, which was sufficiently long ago that a variety of aspects of performance would have been recorded for recruits who entered in that year. Since over 2,000 officers were appointed in 1957, our sample size is large enough to permit distinguishing the characteristics of subgroups that are small on a percentage basis: black officers, promoted officers, detectives, etc.

Our objectives were as follows:

1. To develop information on how to select men likely to perform effectively as police officers and to reject candidates likely to be unsatisfactory.
2. To identify attributes currently thought to be negative or positive indicators which in fact are not related to later good or poor performance.
3. To identify methods for sharpening the estimate of a recruit's future performance by using information from his probationary period on the force, and for determining which probationary patrolmen should be terminated.
4. To determine the kind of men who are likely to perform ineffectively in areas in which complaints against policemen are common.

1

In the next chapter we review, in some detail, the background to this study, including the important issues and the previously completed research. Then, in Chapter 3, we describe the methodology and the data used in the study. The distinctions between officers who leave the department and those who stay, and the differences between black and white officers, are also discussed in this chapter. In Chapter 4, we present our findings in regard to all the significant relationships of each background characteristic to later dimensions of perform-ance, which were primarily derived from cross-tabulations. In Chapter 5, we describe the results of our regression analysis, which identified the combinations of background characteristics most strongly associated with each performance measure and quantified the strength of the relationship. Finally, in Chapter 6, we present typical profiles of the characteristics of officers having specified patterns of performance.

Background to the Study

In most U.S. cities, policemen are appointed through a civil service procedure in which candidates must meet certain objective standards, usually established by law, and they must pass a written civil service examination and a medical examination. In addition, some cities use subjective criteria based on personal interviews, psychiatric examinations, or background investigations. As an illustration, the criteria which apply for appointment as a patrolman in New York City are shown in Table 2-1.

Major open questions about police selection are whether the standards now in use, either individually or collectively, actually distinguish the candidates who will become successful policemen from those who will not, and whether the

Table 2-1
Criteria for Appointment—NYPD

Objective Criteria	Requirement
Citizenship	U.S.
Age	At least 21 when appointed No more than 29 at application (year-for-year waiver for military service)
Residency	No requirement. When appointed, must live in one of 11 N.Y. counties
Education	High school graduate or equivalent
Height	At least 5'7"
Vision	20/30 each eye, without glasses
Drivers License	Yes
Criminal History	No felony or petty larceny conviction
Military History	No dishonorable discharge
Examinations	
Mental	Grade of 75 or better on written civil service exam
Medical/Physical	"Good physical condition"
Subjective Criteria	
Background investigation	"Proof of good character" (Rejections subject to review by two hearing boards)

addition or substitution of new selection instruments can improve the predictive validity of the selection process. In addition, the question of whether the selection procedures discriminate against members of minority groups is being raised with increasing frequency.

Although many studies have been undertaken in an attempt to answer these questions, they remain far from resolved, mainly for the following reasons:

1. No entirely satisfactory method has been developed to measure objectively the performance of policemen once appointed; those performance measures in use tend to reflect the internal standards of police departments rather than the requirements of the community being served.

2. Within any given police department, there are a variety of functions to be performed, ranging from traffic control and patrol in low crime areas to undercover activities, crime investigation, operation of data processing systems, planning, supervision of other officers, and administration. Some men who are able to perform certain of these functions extremely well may be unsuited for other tasks, and the selection process must provide appropriate numbers of personnel to fill all positions.

3. If a substantial change in selection criteria is contemplated, one would like to be able to estimate the expected change in performance levels. But it is rarely possible to find a sample of appointed officers who failed to meet existing standards, and the number of men in a given department who might meet a set of higher standards is likely to be so small as to prohibit statistically significant findings.

4. Many researchers believe that the primary influences on an individual's performance as a policeman are encountered subsequent to his appointment. These factors include the training process, socialization by fellow officers, the nature of the community in precincts of early assignments, and happenstances of acquaintance with officers who later rise to high command positions. If such later influences are in fact of major importance, then observed relationships between background characteristics and police performance measures can be artifacts of existing assignment procedures. For example, young recruits may be initially assigned as foot patrolmen in high crime areas more frequently than older recruits, and officers who perform well in high crime areas may later be eligible for appointment as plainclothes investigators. A comparison of age at appointment with ultimate assignment might then suggest that older men do not become satisfactory plainclothesmen, whereas this conclusion would actually be unwarranted from the data.

5. The findings of the studies themselves have in some cases been so ambiguous or negative as to preclude the possibility of drawing conclusions of practical use for improving selection or assignment procedures. Indeed, some of the findings are bizarre when viewed from the perspective

of selection criteria. For example, Singer[2] has remarked that a 1950 study[3] of 25 New York policemen can be interpreted as showing that one can identify successful policemen as men who have low aspirations and are socially maladjusted.

6. The nature of police work differs substantially from one jurisdiction to another, so that findings in a given city are not necessarily applicable elsewhere.

Despite these limitations, some progress has been made toward clarifying the relationship between the background characteristics of police candidates and their later performance. Of the many studies[4-32] that we reviewed in preparing this work, we have chosen eighteen[4-21] for discussion here as being typical of those using actual data on the background and performance of some sample of officers. The predictor variables and the performance variables used in these studies are displayed in Tables 2-2 and 2-3. The most commonly used predictors have been scores on some collection of personality, aptitude, or mechanical tests. Although these are shown together on Table 2-2 as a single item, several of the studies utilized a large number of such variables.

For example, Baehr, Furcon, and Froemel[4] administered seventeen different paper-and-pencil tests to the subjects in their study, thereby measuring a total of 121 variables. In the study reported by Blum,[5] police recruits completed four tests: the Minnesota Multiphasic Personality Inventory (MMPI), the group form of the Rorschach Ink Blot Test, the Strong Vocational Inventory Blank, and the "F" scale for measurement of authoritarian trends.

Other commonly used predictor variables have been educational level, some aspect of previous employment history, and age at appointment. Six of the studies used predictor variables from only one or two of the categories shown in Table 2-2.

Among the most frequently utilized performance criteria was termination of employment as a policeman (voluntary or involuntary). In four of the studies,[8, 15, 16, 21] termination of employment was the sole criterion of performance. These studies reflect the belief that officers who terminate have proved unsuited for police work, or that it is desirable for the selection process to assist in reducing training and turnover costs by weeding out those candidates who will not become permanent employees. By far the most thorough and interesting work on termination of employment by police officers has been conducted by Levy.[15, 16] She used samples of thousands of officers from several different departments.

Levy's main findings were that officers who terminate voluntarily are considerably different in background characteristics from those who are terminated for cause, or whose resignations were requested, and both of these groups differ from those who remain on the force. The men who terminate voluntarily were found to be younger at time of appointment and to have more education,

Table 2-2
Previous Studies: Predictor Variables

	Baehr, et al	Blum	Collins	Colarelli, et al	Cross & Hammond	DuBois & Watson	Eilbert	Hankey	Hogan	Humm & Humm	Levy	Marsh	McAllister	Mullineaux	Spencer & Nichols	Valla	Cohen & Chaiken
Personality, Aptitude, Mechanical Tests																	
Standard	x	x	x	x		x	x	x	x	x		x			x		
Developed for police						x	x								x		
Interview														x			
Mental Tests																	
IQ		x															x
Civil Service								x				x	x	x			x
Other				x			x	x						x			
Educational Level	*			x				x			x	x			x		x
Employment History																	
Number or duration of jobs	*										x					x	x
Type of previous employment	*			x				x			x	x					x
Disciplinary record or discharge											x					x	x
Experience in law enforcement								x			x						
Military Record																	
Served				x							x				x	x	x
Highest Rank											x				x		
Disciplinary record																	x
Age at appointment	*							x			x	x			x		x
Marital status or history	*										x				x		x
Violation of Law																	
Motor vehicle and minor											x						x
Arrest for crime																x	x
Possesses drivers license															x		
Hobbies, social activities	*			x													
Debts	*										x						x
Background investigation rating														x			x
Other background (residences, children, parents, health, etc.)	*										x	x			x	x	x
Race	x														x		x

*Data obtained as part of "Personal History Index."

Table 2-3
Previous Studies: Performance Variables

	Baehr, et al	Blum	Collins	Colarelli, et al	Cross & Hammond	DuBois & Watson	Eilbert	Hankey	Hogan	Humm & Humm	Levy	Marsh	McAllister	Mullineaux	Spencer & Nichols	Valla	Cohen & Chaiken
Tenure																	
Termination					X			X		X	X	X	X			X	X
Termination for cause								X			X	X	X				
Training*																	
Grade in police academy						X		X					X	X			X
Instructor's evaluation								X	X								
Student peer rating								X									
Marksmanship						X											X
Supervisory Evaluation																	
Probationary evaluation*						X			X				X	X			X
Later evaluation	X			X			X	X					X	X	X	X	†
Career Development																	
Evaluation for promotion						X		X									
Assignment progression		X															X
Promotion										X							
Accidents																	
Automobile											X						
Personal Injury		X											X	X			X
Invalid claim of injury																	X
Commendations																	
Departmental	X	X						X					X	X			X
From public		X						X									
Absenteeism																	
Number of times sick		X											X				X
Total days sick		X											X				X
Total absences	X													X			
Disciplinary Charges																	
Infractions of departmental rules	X	X	X					X					X	X			X
Serious misconduct		X															X
Civilian complaints																	X
Harassment																	X
Number of Arrests	X			X											X		†

*Considered as predictor variables in some studies
†Detectives only

shorter tenure on immediately previous jobs, and fewer years of residence in the city of application than the other officers. Men who terminate as failures had a history of a larger number of jobs per year, were more likely to have been dismissed from a job, were more likely to have been married more than once, and had a larger number of residences than the other officers. Military and financial data were not found to be related to subsequent termination. In regard to the finding that men who remain on police forces are less educated than those who leave, Levy noted that "it should not be interpreted to mean that poor education insures retention, [but it] may be generated by the fact that Police Departments, in general, do not sufficiently meet the needs of their better educated officers. The better educated officer who meets the needs of his department may leave for more challenging employment."[16]

A second commonly used performance criterion was some form of supervisory evaluation. In cases where the police department under study regularly collected performance ratings, these scores were obtained by the researchers.[4, 12, 20] However, in most instances when performance ratings were used, it was necessary for the researchers to design and administer their own instrument for obtaining the supervisory evaluations.

The most sophisticated method used to determine supervisors' evaluations of performance was the paired-comparison test developed by Baehr, et al.[4] Each sergeant or lieutenant who was acquainted with the performance of at least ten of the patrolmen under study was asked to consider each pair of officers and answer the question, "Which of these two men is the better performer on the street—which is the better patrolman in terms of performance in the field?" Each rater's collection of comparisons was measured for consistency,[a] and raters with consistency levels below 80 percent were excluded from the study. In addition, the ratings produced by different supervisors were compared, and raters whose level of agreement was too low were also excluded. The remaining rankings were converted to normalized scores and averaged for each patrolman under study.

The subjects in the Baehr, Furcon, Froemel (BFF) study were 409 patrolmen, out of 2327 eligible, in the Chicago Police Department who were selected in accordance with their scores on the paired-comparison rating and who agreed to participate. All levels of tenure were represented in the sample, from recent recruits to the most experienced patrolmen, but higher-ranking officers were not included. The paper-and-pencil tests used in this study were administered during the study period. The results of regression analysis of all the test scores against each performance variable showed that multiple correlations above 0.6 could be obtained for the paired-comparison rating and the police department's performance rating. The study did not indicate precisely which relationships attained

---

[a]In the words of the study, "if a rater selects patrolman A over patrolman B, and patrolman B over patrolman C, then to be consistent, he should also select A over C. If he selects C over A, this choice is regarded as an inconsistency."

statistical significance. The multiple correlation coefficient for prediction of absenteeism, disciplinary actions, and departmental awards were typically lower, in the neighborhood of 0.5. The authors concluded that there were "significant and acceptably high relationships between the tests and all eight of the performance criterion measures used." The predictors having the strongest correlations, consistent among subjects, were elements of background and experience derived from a Personal History Index, a cooperativeness variable from a test of social insight, and temperament traits of self-confidence and self-starting (positive) and demonstrativeness (negative).

The Chicago study also found that when the officers were divided into subgroups according to race, some important differences appeared in the relationship between test scores and performance measures. For example, among the personal history variables used, the dimension Early Family Responsibility was positively related to the paired-comparison rating, and the variable Selling Experience was negatively related, for both blacks and whites, while positive weights for Parental Family Adjustment and Professional Successful Parents and a negative weight for School Achievement were found for whites only, and negative weights for Financial Responsibility and Leadership were found for blacks only. On the basis of these and other differences by race observed in the study, BFF recommended "separate validations for different racial groups . . . as a routine procedure in the selection of patrolmen."

Some important characteristics of the BFF study that distinguish it from the present work are the following. First, the tests used by BFF to measure personality and background characteristics were administered to the officers at the time of the study and therefore may reflect attitudes and selective memory of the past induced by on-the-job experiences. In the present study, background characteristics of the subjects were recorded at the time of application and were checked for accuracy by policemen assigned to background investigations. Second, BFF did not use any variables having the property that a specified ranking is a prerequisite for appointment; these include such potentially interesting variables as civil service examination scores, which are used in the present study. Third, the subjects of the BFF study were volunteers, and none of them fell in the middle third of performance, as measured by the paired-comparison rankings. In the present study, every officer who entered the New York City Police Department in 1957 was included as a subject, except for a small number (4 percent) whose records could not be located. In addition to avoiding biases introduced by using volunteers, such a cohort design controls for the variable of tenure (or experience), which had to be treated as a quasi-performance variable by BFF.[b]

The study by Spencer and Nichols[20] was also performed in the Chicago

---

[b]In subsequent studies by these same researchers, tests similar to those used in BFF have been validated with other research designs. In particular, these tests have been administered to applicants. Some of their results appeared after completion of the present study. [33]

Police Department. In this case, a projective design was used, and test scores and background data were obtained at the time of application, which was 1964. The subjects in this study were 427 applicants who survived all steps in the appointment process up to, but not including, the background investigation. Of these, 109 men failed to qualify for appointment after the background investigation. Performance measures were obtained four years later for those subjects who remained on the force, a total of 268 men.

Although Spencer and Nichols used "failure to qualify" as a criterion variable, it is not actually a performance measure, and therefore their findings in regard to this variable are not reported here. Of the remaining criteria used, as shown in Table 2-3, only one was found to be "consistently related to predictor information." This was an average score on the department's semi-yearly performance rating, which had a multiple correlation of .272 with these three variables: 1) a personality rating based on Personal History and Sentence Completion forms, 2) civil service exam score, and 3) level of education. The three variables are listed in the order of their strength as predictors. The fact that this multiple correlation is considerably smaller than those reported by BFF is quite likely explained by differences in research design and in the number of variables used in the multiple regression; it does not necessarily suggest that the predictors used by Spencer and Nichols are less powerful. The directions of the relationships were as one would expect: departmental performance ratings increased with the personality rating, civil service score, and education.

With regard to differences by race, Spencer and Nichols observed that, on the average, blacks had lower performance ratings than whites. But the personality ratings used in this study, while good predictors of performance, were found to have a "relatively low relationship with race, compared with the civil service examination and other predictors." This pair of observations is somewhat paradoxical but does appear to suggest that separate validations of predictor variables may not be required for different races. None of the other studies discussed in our summary, aside from the two already described, considered race as a pertinent predictor variable.

The subjects in the Hankey study[12] were 801 policemen in the Los Angeles Police Department who were appointed to the force in the period from 1955 to 1959. All of the background data and personality test scores used as predictor variables in this study were recorded prior to, or within a few weeks after, appointment, and data for the performance measures were collected in 1962. Thus, the performance of the subjects was measured for varying periods of time, ranging from three to eight years.

Hankey's main interest was in determining the predictive power of ten trait scores of the Guilford-Zimmerman Temperament Survey (GZTS). Multiple regression analysis using these ten scores as independent variables and a weighted average of supervisor's evaluations as the dependent variable produced a multiple correlation coefficient which was not significant at the .05 level. Similar findings of nonsignificant predictive value of the GZTS scores were found in a discriminant function analysis in which subjects were divided into success/non-success groups in accordance with scores on each of the following variables taken separately:

1. Recruit training score
2. Average supervisory evaluation
3. Score on sergeant's promotional oral examination
4. Termination of employment
5. Punitive days off.

Indeed, even when predictor variables other than GZTS scores were considered (see Table 2-3), the only significant relationship found in this study was between measures of mental ability and scores of performance in the recruit academy. Hankey concluded that "no evidence was found to support the hypothesis that successful policemen have a different syndrome of personality traits and other variables as compared with non-successful policemen," and "it does not appear that additional refinement in [selection techniques] would result in an increase in effective and a decrease in ineffective or problem employees."

Considering the similarity between many of the predictor and criterion variables used in the Hankey study and those used in the two Chicago studies described above, the remarkable difference in results suggests strongly the perils of assuming that predictors validated in one city will necessarily prove to be useful in other departments.

Even the continued validity over time of findings in a single department cannot be assumed with confidence. This is illustrated by two studies conducted in different years in the Los Angeles Police Department, both of which used an appraisal of the Humm-Wadsworth Temperament Scale as the predictor variable. Unfortunately, the performance criterion differed in the two cases. Humm and Humm,[14] in a study conducted in the 1940s, judged performance to be bad if an officer was dismissed and to be above average if he was eventually appointed to an executive or administrative position. They found extremely strong relationships between Humm-Wadsworth appraisals and this performance criterion. Fifteen years later, Collins[6] compared Humm-Wadsworth scores with punitive days off and found no significant relationships.

The Humm and Humm study is potentially of great interest not only because of the high correlations obtained but also because it describes an instance in which candidates who failed to meet civil service criteria were nonetheless appointed to the force (under war emergency regulations). However, several characteristics of the research design and the sample of subjects selected for this study make the results difficult to interpret, and the published results do not permit drawing conclusions about performance differences between the civil service appointees and the others. One subgroup of the sample was appointed and tested in 1943-44, with follow-up in 1945 to determine which subjects had been dismissed or terminated. A second subgroup consists of men dismissed or terminated between 1946 and 1949, but it is not clear whether this subgroup includes some men in the previous subgroup or at what point in their careers the men in this subgroup were tested. A third subgroup ("staff") consists of men holding administrative or executive positions, many of whom were apparently tested several years after joining the force. In addition, as Blum pointed out,[34] "it appears that among a total of 669 men tested, 79 resigned, 233 were fired, and 357 remained with the department. The ratio of men fired to men resigned is most unusual and suggests a very special situation in the department" at that time.

The results given by Humm and Humm showed that 84.8 percent of the men eventually dismissed had low Humm-Wadsworth (H-W) appraisals, while only 32.2 percent of the staff had such ratings. A cross-tabulation of H-W appraisals vs. the qualities dismissed, average, or staff showed a correlation of .72 and a chi-square measure of significance at a level well below .001. However, Blum pointed out that a reworking of the data from the point of view of predictive validity leads to less impressive results. He concluded that of the men predicted to do badly, 42 percent did well, and of the men expected to do good or fair work, 66 percent did well. Thus, the possible value of temperament measures such as the Humm-Wadsworth scale is left in doubt by both the Humm and Humm study and the one by Collins mentioned earlier.

Two studies in New York City came to negative conclusions consistent with those of Hankey and Collins. However, both of them were characterized by a relatively short follow-up period for measuring performance. Eilbert[11] used a sample of "approximately 1,000 recruits" who were tested in 1962 and the first half of 1963 and whose performance was evaluated in the first quarter of 1964. The predictor variables in this study were derived from a battery of tests developed by the author and his colleagues after a task analysis of police work that identified what they believed to be the critical requirements for good police performance. The wide range of personal background attributes examined in this study is particularly noteworthy. In addition to tests of verbal and visual abilities and personality attributes, this study included tests of knowledge of sports, first aid and safety, "handyman" techniques, city social agencies, *modus operandi* of criminals, New York City points of interest, the law, and police and underworld lingo. The performance criterion was obtained from a specially-developed supervisory evaluation form that required the evaluator to rank the subjects known to him in terms of their estimated performance in twenty critical problem situations and in terms of overall performance. Subjects were labelled either high or low in performance on the basis of these ratings, with rankings obtained from only a single evaluator treated separately from those obtained from two or more.

In this study, predictive validity was measured using biserial correlation coefficients. Most of the specially developed tests were either unreliable or failed to provide a significant difference between high- and low-ranked performers. Exceptions were a vocabulary test "which closely resembles the type of pre-employment tests currently used" and knowledge of foreign terms and police lingo.

The second New York City study, by McAllister,[18] was concerned with the predictive validity of the background investigator's rating, which is a subjective decision arrived at after a personal interview with the candidate and consideration of all available background data. Because the recommendations of the investigators are reviewed by a board of police officers, some applicants may be appointed despite a disapproval by the background investigator. The subjects in this study were 356 men appointed to the New York City Police Department in December 1965, of whom 75 (19 percent) had been disapproved by the background investigator.

Their performance was measured 18 months later, using a specially-developed supervisor's evaluation form and the other performance variables shown in Table 2-3. The evaluator rated each subject on a scale from 1 to 10 ("unsatisfactory" to "outstanding") in regard to alertness, common sense, initiative, integrity, intelligence, and self-reliance, and the total score was used as a performance variable. Analysis was undertaken by cross-tabulation, using a chi-square test of significance. The general conclusion of the study was that the hypothesis of better performance being associated with a favorable judgment by the background investigator was not supported by the data. None of the performance measures was found to be significantly related to the background investigator's rating at the .01 level of significance.[c] However, of five subjects whose services were terminated during the probationary period, four were disapproved by the background investigator. McAllister noted that criterion variables based on sick time were so similarly distributed for approved and disapproved officers that the use of such variables as measures of performance is called into question. He also observed that supervisors' ratings of intelligence and common sense appear to be inversely related to standard I.Q. scores.

The study reported by Blum[5] is notable for the relatively long follow-up period (seven years), and the exclusive use of performance measures commonly found in police personnel folders, not including a subjective overall performance evaluation by supervisors. However, the number of subjects in the study was small (87). The department in which the study was conducted is identified only as "a major metropolitan police force." Personality tests were administered to

---

[c]The results of the present study differ; we attribute this to our use of a longer period for measuring performance rather than to any change in the background investigations between 1957 and 1965.

the officers hired in 1956-57 soon after their appointment, and a performance prognosis score was developed at that time. Performance data were collected in 1963. For each performance measure used (see Table 2-3), its zero-order correlation with each test score was determined. The highest correlations observed (above .40) were found to describe the relationship between certain MMPI tests and subsequent evidence of especially serious misconduct (which was observed for four subjects).

Blum noted that if one had a goal of weeding out all four "bad" men by using their test scores, while minimizing the number of "good" men rejected on the same basis, cutting points could have been set at 32 for the MMPI Schizophrenia subscale and at 28 for the Pt (obsessive-compulsive) score. This would have excluded ten "good" men from appointment in addition to the four others, and five of those ten were subsequently charged with less serious disciplinary infractions. Such conclusions must be viewed as suggestive only, due to the small number of subjects in the "bad" category.

Blum found that correlations of test scores with measures of performance other than misconduct were considerably lower (under .30 in magnitude). He summarized the ones of interest as follows: "Receiving commendations and praise is related to vocational interests, attitudes and orientation, and intelligence. It is not related to personality measures. Being subject to accidents, injury or time off for illness is related to vocational interests, intelligence, personality, and attitudes and orientation." No correlations larger than .22 were found between test scores and termination of employment, and none larger than .14 were found for assignment progression, which was a subjective measure of the merit of a subject's assignment history provided by a police official who was not necessarily familiar with the subject.

The study by Marsh[17] used predictor variables similar to those of Blum (but only the MMPI was identical) plus other personal and biographical data and civil service exam scores. Marsh's subjects were 591 deputy sheriffs in Los Angeles County who were appointed during the period from 1947-50. The tests were administered after selection, but while the men were still recruits. Performance was evaluated in 1957, providing a seven- to ten-year follow-up. The performance criteria, shown in Table 2-3, included a supervisory rating in which subjects were sorted into five categories of overall performance by individual supervisors and the joint evaluations were ranked "high" or "low" (with some subjects not included in either group).

The analysis consisted of comparing predictor variables for "high" vs. "low" subjects and for "high" vs. discharged subjects. None of the reported findings are directly comparable with those of Blum, but the general thrust of the results suggests that no common patterns were found in these two studies. Marsh found that the civil service exam score distinguished good performers from those discharged (with the higher scoring subjects more likely to perform well), and successful performance was predicted by low scores on the MMPI Hypomanic and Hypochondriasis scales and the general activity C scale of the Guilford-Martin Temperament Inventory. Vocational interests, as measured by the Kuder Preference Record, were not significantly related to the performance categories used, but a prior history of experience as a policeman or fireman was an indicator of a low rating as a deputy sheriff. An interesting finding was that men with high civil service scores tended to have shorter tenure, confirming that termination of employment may frequently reflect the opportunities open in other occupations, rather than unsatisfactory performance. This study also produced one of the "bizarre" findings referred to earlier: the height of the subject was found to be significantly related to the probability of discharge at the .01 level.

The remaining studies shown in the tables will be summarized briefly. Colarelli and Siegel,[7] in a study of the Kansas State Highway Patrol, found that candidates who were later rated unsatisfactory had a large difference between language and nonlanguage scores on an I.Q. test, enjoyed the authority of the badge and uniform, and had scores outside the normal range on four specified MMPI scales. DuBois and Watson,[9] in a St. Louis study, used criteria of performance primarily based on very short follow-up periods (e.g., recruit training score, marksmanship, and service rating after ten weeks). Such variables ought more properly to be considered predictors, since in most departments it is not difficult to dismiss recruits who show signs of becoming unsuccessful policemen. DuBois later used evaluations for promotion as a performance measure,[10] and recruit academy grade was designated a valid predictor, along with certain paper-and-pencil tests. Mullineaux[19] also had a brief evaluation period in his 1955 study of the Baltimore City Police Department. Recruits were rated by captains on a five-level scale at the end of three and six months. The main conclusion of this study was that the ability to write legible, correctly spelled reports was a factor in later performance, but was not measured in any of the qualifying tests.

The most recent prediction study using a brief evaluation period was conducted by Hogan.[13] His subjects were either in their final stages of training at the Maryland State Police Academy, or they had one year's field experience. The subjects were given the California Psychological Inventory and were rated by a supervisor on either overall suitability for police work or actual job performance. Hogan obtained a multiple correlation of 0.42 between scores on scales of his predictor test and the supervisory evaluation.

General conclusions that can be drawn from previously completed studies of the relationship of background and personality characteristics to police performance are the following:

1. Many variables that would appear logically related to police performance do not prove to be valid predictors of performance. This was demonstrated

especially by Eilbert's study, in which tests were specifically constructed for their apparent relation to police performance.

2. A few standard psychological and personality tests may be valuable as predictors of very bad performance (e.g., dismissal for cause), but they do not appear to be as useful for identifying effective long-term performance.

3. Personal history data have frequently emerged as better predictors of both good and bad performance than written test scores of any kind.

4. The nature of the relationship between predictors and performance is likely to depend on the race of the subjects.

5. In order to develop predictors of general utility, it will be necessary for a systematic program of validation studies to be conducted over a period of years with similar research designs in several cities. Otherwise, the conflicting findings now in the literature are not likely to be clarified.

In the present study, we have analyzed the predictive power of personal history data of a type commonly available to police departments without the administration of any special tests. Our research design could be readily applied in any major city, using its present personnel files. In light of the findings presented above, we have been particularly concerned with background attributes that are currently used and thought to be important in accepting or rejecting applicants but that may not be related to subsequent performance. Therefore, we have not excluded variables whose values are truncated by virtue of existing selection procedures.

In two respects we have been able to address certain questions essentially untouched in previously reported work. First, because of our long follow-up period (11 years), we have been able to test the predictive power of early performance measures such as recruit training score and probationary evaluations. The objective here is to enable police departments to select the recruits for appointment to permanent positions in the force on the basis of a combination of background characteristics and data collected during the probationary period. Second, we have an extensive file of all civilian complaints and allegations of harassment against officers in our sample; these provide two separate (albeit negative) measures of performance from the point of view of the community and enable us to identify the characteristics of officers who probably are unsatisfactory for assignment in sensitive areas of our cities.

Other characteristics of the present study that distinguish it from previously completed ones are the following:

1. All the subjects were officers in a single police department, and yet the sample size is large enough to study interesting subgroups such as black officers, detectives, and college-educated men. In particular, we are able to analyze the need for separate validation of predictors by race.

2. All the subjects entered the Police Department in a single year.

3. Nearly every officer who entered the Department in the selected year is included as a subject. There was no need to request men to volunteer to cooperate with the study, and thus such biases as may be introduced through the use of volunteers were not present.
4. We did not confine our study to officers of a particular rank. In fact, the entire range from patrolman to captain is represented in the sample. Thus, it is possible to use career advancement as a measure of performance.

3

Research Design and Description of Variables

This study is based on a cohort research design, a technique which is described and justified in some detail by Wolfgang, Figlio, and Sellin.[35] In general, a cohort refers to a group of people who have experienced the same event at the same point in time. In our case, all the subjects of this study were appointed to the New York City Police Department in the same year, 1957. The use of a cohort design automatically standardizes for the tenure of the officers and assures that they all experienced a similar sequence of departmental policies in regard to assignment and promotion. Our choice of the year 1957 was based on the fact that a large number of officers were appointed in that year and on our desire to collect performance data covering at least a ten-year period.

To be precise, our cohort consists of all male officers appointed in 1957, except for those whose files giving background or performance information could not be located in 1968. Of the 2,002 men appointed in 1957, 1,626 (81 percent) remained on the force in 1968, and the background records were located for all but 18 of these (1 percent). Thus, our "active" cohort consists of 1,608 subjects appointed in 1957 and followed up 11 years later.

The remaining 376 officers had left the force prior to 1968, due to resignation, dismissal, or death. We were less successful in locating files for these men, since they had in most cases been removed from storage in the unit where they had been filled out. We obtained records for 307 men who were appointed in 1957 and whose employment was terminated prior to 1968; they constitute the "inactive" cohort for this study. Because we cannot be sure that the missing 69 inactives were not "special" in some way, and because performance data for the inactives do not cover comparable periods of time, we have devoted most of our attention in the chapters which follow to analysis of the active cohort. In this chapter, however, we describe the important differences between the actives and inactives for whom we have data. We have not distinguished the officers who were terminated for cause from the other inactives, since in many cases the cause of termination was unclear from the records.

Nearly all data on background and performance of the subjects were collected in late 1968; the rank of the active officers was updated in 1971. A small number of men (8) terminated between 1968 and 1971. They were included in this study as members of the active cohort, and their rank was updated to the highest level attained prior to termination. The background data were obtained from records completed in 1957 or earlier, and thus represent the best information about the candidate available to the Police Department during the selection process. Many of the items of background information were verified for accuracy by the Department's background investigators.

Data Analysis

The relations between predictor variables and individual performance measures, as well as the relations among the performance measures taken as a group, were first determined from cross-tabulations and simple correlations. These tabulations were obtained separately for the black officers and the total active cohort, which predominantly consists of white officers. The initial rationale was to avoid summary analyses based on large linear combinations of either predictor or performance measures. The absence of a fully developed theory or model of how individual predictor variables are related to each performance variable required that we examine a large number of such relationships.

Several criteria for assessing the importance and reliability of these relationships were used. These include: the internal consistency of associations; the conformability of the associations with belief and knowledge of experienced people in this field; and formal statistical tests such as chi-square and F tests. The computer program used throughout this research was the Statistical Package for the Social Sciences (SPSS).

In the next part of our study, we identified those variables showing a substantial association with performance measures, and we factor-analyzed our data for black officers and for the total active cohort. The factor analysis for the active cohort was based upon 37 of the background and performance measures, while the analysis for the black subcohort was based upon 32 of them. We used factor analysis as a descriptive technique to identify groups of performance variables that would tend to have similar relationships with background. This helped us determine which measures of police performance in this study reflected different dimensions of behavior resulting from different sources of variations.

The results of the cross-tabulations, zero-order correlations, and factor analysis led to hypotheses for predicting performance from background variables. These hypotheses were then tested using step-wise multiple regression analysis. We selected this technique of analysis as our primary statistical tool for developing a prediction instrument for the following reasons: unlike other simpler techniques (e.g., the Biographical Inventory Blank), multiple regression analysis does not require that we devise a preliminary scoring system, and it is also a widely recognized statistical procedure. Moreover, the relative impact of items may be compared through computation of their standardized regression coefficients.

After we identified which predictor variables and combinations of these variables had the strongest correlations with performance of the black and white officers, we compared the results with the criteria traditionally used for selecting recruits. From the regression analysis, we were able to identify the combination of individual background factors that provides the most powerful indication of later measures of performance.

Sources of Data

Data were collected manually from the files of many different units within the Police Department by research assistants under our personal supervision. The Department placed no restrictions on the items of data to be recorded by us, and we selected over 150 descriptors for each subject, not all of which were analyzed in the study. A complete set of the code sheets is shown in Appendix A. The subjects are identified by a code number in our files, so it is no longer possible for us to connect any data with a particular officer by name. The data were collected in the main from the following units:[a]

1. Chief Clerk's Personnel Unit. This unit contains personnel and detailed personal data on each officer's background and performance in the Department, including his promotions and history of assignments. It also contains information resulting from the character investigation at the time of application to the Department.

2. Disciplinary Record Unit. Contains all complaints leveled against police officers that resulted in charges and specifications and a departmental trial. Awards won by officers are also filed here.

3. Medical Unit. Contains a detailed medical history of each officer.

4. Counseling Unit. Contains the results of psychological and I.Q. tests.

5. Public Morals Unit. Contains a record of the vast majority of complaints of corruption that came to the attention of the Department.

6. Personnel Record Unit. Contains detailed information on each officer's education and specialized skills.

7. Detective Division. Contains more detailed information on detectives. This includes a record of all felony and misdemeanor arrests made by detectives, as well as individual performance ratings.

8. Civilian Complaint Review Board. Contains all complaints against officers of unnecessary force, brutality, abuse of authority, discourteous behavior, or

[a]The locations of some files and the names of some units may have changed since 1968.

ethnic slurs. Detailed records pertaining to the investigation of these complaints are also maintained here.

9. Chief Inspector's Investigating Unit. Contains records of selected charges of corruption and departmental complaints against police officers.

10. Limited Duty Section. Contains data pertaining to men assigned to limited duty, including the reason for this assignment.

11. Old Record Section. Contains data on men who left the force (and also candidates who applied and were either rejected or declined the invitation to join the force).

12. Background Investigation and Screening Unit. Contains detailed personal information resulting from character probes conducted by specially trained police investigators before the officer is accepted as a member of the force.

13. Police Academy Reports. Contains records of performance of each officer while he was a recruit in the Police Academy.

Predictor Variables

The background and early performance variables actually used in this study are described below and summarized at the end of this chapter.

Race and Age

1. Race. The race of the subject was determined from a photograph attached to his application, on the back of which a notation had been made of the applicant's race. Of the 1,608 actives, 1,484 (92.2 percent) were white, 99 (6.2 percent) were black, and 25 (1.55 percent) were Hispanic.[b] Of the 307 inactives, 286 (93.1 percent) were white, 19 (6.2 percent) were black, and 2 (0.7 percent) were Hispanic. There were evidently no differential patterns of termination by race.

2. Age. This is the subject's age at time of appointment, which was determined approximately by subtracting his year of birth from 1957. The average age of all subjects was 25.7 years, with blacks slightly older (average 26.7 years). Due to

[b]Due to the small sample size for Hispanics, the distributions of other variables are not presented separately for this subgroup. However, Hispanics are included in tabulations for the total active cohort.

appointment requirements, none of the men was under 21, and the 10.4 percent who were 30 or older were all military veterans.

Mental Examinations

3. I.Q. This score was obtained from the Otis Self-Administering Test of Mental Ability, Higher Examination: Form D, which was administered to the subjects when they were recruits. The distribution of I.Q. scores for the active cohort is shown in Table 3-1. The average I.Q. for blacks was 102.3 and for all others was 104.4, but the difference of the distributions was found to be not significant, using a chi-square test at the .05 level. The I.Q. scores of a large number of inactives were not located, and therefore we cannot compare them with the actives on this variable.

4. Civil Service. This is the grade on a standard written examination for appointment as a patrolman that was developed, administered, and scored by the New York City Department of Personnel. Candidates who are military veterans are eligible for extra points which raise their position on the appointment list, but these points have not been included in the grade recorded for this variable. Not all the subjects took exactly the same examination. However, 85 percent of the subjects took either the 1956 or the 1957 examination; in those years, the passing grade was 70.

Civil Service is the only variable in this study for which data were not available in Police Department files and for which data for inactives were not obtained. The distribution of civil service scores by race is shown in Table 3-2.

Table 3-1
I.Q. Scores–Actives

I.Q.	Black		White	
	Number	Percent	Number	Percent
<90	1	1.1	42	2.9
90- 99	29	30.5	353	24.4
100-109	44	46.3	669	46.3
110-119	19	20.0	303	21.0
120+	2	2.1	79	5.5
Total	95	100.0	1,446	100.0
Unknown	4		38	
Average	102.3		104.4	

Differences by race are not significant.

Table 3-2
Civil Service Written Exam Scores—Actives

Grade	Blacks		All Others	
	Number	Percent	Number	Percent
Under 75	39	41.1	525	36.8
75-79.9	36	37.9	547	38.0
80-84.9	15	15.8	243	16.8
85+	5	5.3	124	8.4
Total	95	100.0	1,439	100.0
Unknown	4		70	
Average		76.3		77.1

Differences by race are not significant.

The average scores for blacks and whites were almost equal, with the difference in the means not significant at the .05 level, and the difference in the distributions definitely not significant: $\chi^2 = 1.762$ with 3 d.f., $p > .5$. Thus we do not find that the fraction of blacks in any particular range of scores (e.g., under 75) is *significantly* different from the fraction of whites in this range.

Family Descriptors

5. Family Mental Disorder. This is the number of immediate members of the subject's family who had a history of mental disorder at the time of application, as recorded by the applicant on his application form. Some 7.7 percent of the actives listed one or more members of their family who had a history of mental disorder. No significant difference appeared by race or active/inactive status.

6. Region of Birth. This was coded into seven categories that were collapsed into two for this study. Those subjects born in New York City were coded 0 on this variable; all others were coded 1. As can be seen in Table 3-3, substantially fewer whites were born outside New York City than other races. No differences were observed between actives and inactives.

7. Siblings. The number of siblings averaged 2.5 ± 0.1 for all subgroups.

8. Father's Occupation. The actual occupation as recorded by the subject on his application was converted to a scale of occupational prestige, with scores ranging from 0 to 100, given by the Socio-Economic Index for Occupations developed by Otis D. Duncan.[36] Occupations ranking highest on this scale were

25

Table 3-3
Region of Birth—Total Cohort

	Black		White		Hispanic	
Region	Number	Percent	Number	Percent	Number	Percent
NYC	84	71.2	1,662	93.9	21	77.8
Other U.S.	34	28.8	108	6.1	6	22.2
Total	118	100.0	1,770	100.0	27	100.0

Distribution for whites is significantly different from the others.

considered to be the most prestigious, usually requiring the most education and providing the highest salaries. If the subject's father was deceased or absent, his mother's occupation was coded. The white applicants' fathers had jobs rating higher on this scale than those of black applicants. Inactives did not differ from actives on this variable, as shown in Table 3-4.

Occupational History

9. Last Occupation. This is the subject's occupation, scored as for the preceding variable, in the position he held immediately before joining the police force. The

Table 3-4
Socio-Economic Index of Father's Occupation—Actives

Socio-Economic Index	Black		White	
	Number	Percent	Number	Percent
00-09	35	35.4	333	22.4
10-19	29	29.3	358	24.1
20-29	9	9.1	210	14.2
30-39	11	11.1	240	16.2
40-49	7	7.1	184	12.4
50-59	4	4.0	59	4.0
60-69	3	3.0	59	4.0
70-79	0	–	12	0.8
80-89	1	1.0	19	1.3
90-99	0	–	10	0.7
Total	99	100.0	1,484	100.0
Average	20.1		25.3	

Differences in averages and in the distributions (when grouped) are significant at the .05 level.

Table 3-5
Socio-Economic Index of Subject's Last Occupation—Actives

Socio-Economic Index	Black		White	
	Number	Percent	Number	Percent
00-09	5	5.1	99	6.7
10-19	15	15.2	251	16.9
20-29	20	20.2	261	17.6
30-39	11	11.1	204	13.7
40-49	38	38.4	396	33.4
50-59	4	4.0	101	6.8
60-69	5	5.1	59	4.0
70-79	1	1.0	5	0.3
80-89	0	–	6	0.4
90-99	0	–	2	0.1
Total	99	100.0	1,484	100.0
Average	34.6		33.8	

Differences by race are not significant.

distribution for actives is shown in Table 3-5. No differences were observed by race or active/inactive status.

10. Jobs. This is a count of the number of positions listed by the subject on his application in response to the request, "List . . . each and every place in which you were employed. . . . (Include all part-time employment.)" The average number of jobs held by actives was 5.7, assuming that "8 or more" averages 9 jobs, with no differences by race. In Table 3-6, we see that inactives were found to have a larger number of previous jobs, significant at the .001 level by chi-square test.

11. Employment Disciplinary Record. This is a count of the number of employers listed by the subject on his application, in response to the questions, "Were you ever discharged or asked to resign from employment?" and "Were you ever subjected to disciplinary action in connection with any employment?" This information was checked by the Police Department's background investigator. Twelve percent of the actives and 14 percent of the inactives had one or more instances of employment discipline; the difference is not significant at the .05 level. There were no differences by race. The overall distribution of this variable is shown in Table 3-7.

Table 3-6
Number of Previous Jobs–Total Cohort

	Inactives		Actives	
Jobs	Number	Percent	Number	Percent
None	1	0.0	6	0.0
1	12	3.9	53	3.3
2	15	4.9	95	5.9
3	34	11.1	212	13.3
4	30	9.8	241	15.0
5	33	10.8	230	14.4
6	30	9.8	180	11.3
7	24	7.8	157	9.8
8+	127	41.5	425	26.6
Total	306	100.0	1,599	100.0
Average*		6.3		5.7

*Assuming the average in the category "8+" was 9.
The distributions are significantly different, when grouped.
(χ^2 = 30.3 with 7 d.f., $p < .001$)

Table 3-7
Employment Disciplinary Record–Total Cohort

Employment Disciplinary Record	Number	Percent
0	1675	87.5
1	191	10.0
2	32	1.7
3	6	0.3
4	4	0.2
5	1	0.1
6	0	–
7	0	–
8	1	0.1
Unknown	5	0.3
Total	1915	100.0
Average	.16	

Military History

12. Military Record. This variable was given the value 1 if the subject served in the armed forces, and 0 otherwise. A greater proportion of actives (83.4 percent) than inactives (77.9 percent) had a military record (significant at the .05 level of chi-square), but no differences by race were observed. The large fraction of veterans in the cohort is typical of the post-Korean War years.

13. Military Discipline. This is a count of items listed by the subject on his application in response to the question, "Were you ever courtmartialed, tried on charges, or were you the subject of a summary court, deck court, captain's mast or company punishment, or any other disciplinary action?" This information was corrected, if necessary, by the background investigator, who had access to the applicant's military file. Approximately 32 percent of applicants (of all races) with a military record had one or more such disciplinary actions. The inactives did not differ significantly from actives in this regard. See Table 3-8 for the overall distribution of this variable.

14. Military Commendations. This is a zero-one variable indicating whether the background investigator listed any military commendations under "Special merit for approval," after reviewing the subject's military file. Among the 1,231 actives who had a military record, 476 (35.5 percent) had military commendations, while of 239 veterans who became inactives, only 62 (25.9 percent) had commendations. Thus, the men who had military commendations were less likely to leave the force; this difference was significant at the .01 level.

Table 3-8
Military Disciplinary Record—Total Cohort

Military Discipline	Number	Percent
Does not apply	335	17.5
None	1094	57.1
1	349	18.2
2	91	4.8
3	26	1.4
4	10	0.5
5	6	0.3
6	3	0.2
Unknown	1	0.1
Total	1915	100.0
Average		.37

Personal History

15. Residences. This is a count of the number of addresses listed by the subject on his application in response to the instruction ". . . state each and every place in which you have resided since you left elementary school. . . ." If military addresses were listed, they were not counted. Inactives and actives both averaged about 2.6 on this variable, with blacks having significantly more residences (average 3.4). This may be related to the observation that more black subjects than whites were born outside New York City.

16. Marital Status. This variable takes the values zero and one, with subjects who were married at time of application being coded 1. At the time of application, 48.9 percent of the subjects who remained on the force were married, while only 39.7 percent of those who became inactives were married; this difference is significant at the .005 level by chi-square test with Yates' correction. A slightly larger fraction of blacks than whites were married, but the difference was not significant at the .05 level.

17. Children. This is the number of the subjects' children at the time of application. Among married subjects, the actives had an average of 1.0 children at the time of application; the inactives, 0.75. The differences in the distributions for actives vs. inactives was significant at the .001 level. Married black subjects had slightly more children than whites, but the difference was not significant.

18. Debts. This is a count of the number of items listed by the applicant in response to the question, "Have you any loan, debt, garnishee, wage assignment, or judgment pending against you?" Blacks had more debts than whites, which may be related to the finding that slightly more blacks were married and that they also had slightly larger families than the white subjects. Actives also had more debts than inactives, significant at the .05 level. These findings are shown in Table 3-9.

19. Psychological Disorder. This records whether the subject had any prior history of mental or nervous disorder at the time of application, as indicated by him on his application form in response to the question, "Have you ever had, or been examined for, or treated for, a nervous or mental disorder by a private physician, or at a clinic, hospital, sanitarium or other institution, or while in the military or naval service?" Among the actives, 1.8 percent answered yes. No significant differences were observed for blacks or inactives.

20. Education. The highest level of education recorded by the subject on his application was coded into the categories shown in Table 3-10. Those applicants who were coded as "less than high school" were required to obtain at least a

Table 3-9
Number of Debts at Application—Total Cohort

Debts	Active Blacks		Active Whites		All Actives		All Inactives	
	Number	Percent	Number	Percent	Number	Percent	Number	Percent
0	48	48.5	972	65.5	1,033	64.2	225	73.3
1	18	18.2	342	23.0	367	22.8	57	18.6
2	17	17.2	113	7.6	135	8.4	18	5.9
3	10	10.1	43	2.9	53	3.3	7	2.3
4+	6	6.1	13	0.9	20	1.2	0	—
Total	99	100.0	1,484	100.0	1,608	100.0	307	100.0
Average	1.11		.51		.55		.37	

Average and distribution for blacks are significantly different from those for whites.
Average and distribution for actives are significantly different from those for inactives.

high school equivalency diploma prior to appointment. The black subjects were found to be better educated than the whites, and the inactives were better educated than the actives. It is particularly noteworthy that one-third of the college graduates appointed in 1957 became inactives.

Incidents Involving Police and Courts

21. Arrest History. This is a count of the number of items listed on the application in response to the instruction, "Indicate below all arrests including Juvenile Delinquent, Youthful Offender, Wayward Minor." This information was provided in the first instance by the subject, but it was updated or corrected, if necessary, by the background investigator. On this variable, 9.1 percent of the subjects scored one or more; 1.4 percent scored 2 or more. Table 3-11 shows that no differences were observed by race or active/inactive status on the variable Arrest History. Only 2.2 percent of the subjects had ever been convicted of a non-juvenile offense. These would necessarily be minor offenses, since no police officers are appointed with a *conviction* for a felony or for certain specified misdemeanors.

22. Offense Type. This is a nominal variable. Each incident counted in "Arrest History" was classified into one of the following four categories:

a. Violent offense. Examples: Homicide, rape, aggravated assault and battery.

b. Property offense. Examples: Robbery, burglary, larceny, auto theft.

c. Juvenile-status offense. Examples: Curfew violation, truancy, runaway, incorrigibility.

Table 3-10
Educational Level at Appointment—Total Cohort

Education	Active Blacks		Active Whites		All Actives		All Inactives	
	Number	Percent	Number	Percent	Number	Percent	Number	Percent
0. Less than High School	3	3	72	5	76	5	12	4
1. High School Equivalency Diploma	18	18	376	25	402	25	56	18
2. High School Graduate	39	39	716	48	765	48	174	57
3. Some College	34	34	297	20	337	21	56	18
4. Associate Degree	3	3	9	1	12	1	0	–
5. College Graduate	2	2	14	1	16	1	8	.3
Total	99	100	1,484	100	1,608	100	306	100

When distributions are grouped ($\leqslant$ 1, 2, 3, 4+), the following differences are significant at the .05 level: Black-white and active-inactive.

Table 3-11
Arrest History—Total Cohort

Arrest History	All Actives		All Inactives	
	Number	Percent	Number	Percent
0	1,472	91.5	274	89.3
1	115	7.1	27	8.8
2	14	0.8	6	2.0
3	7	0.4	—	—
Total	1,608	100.0	307	100.0
Average	.10		.13	

Differences are not significant.

d. Other. Examples: Disorderly conduct, possession of a dangerous weapon, narcotics possession, malicious mischief, "violation."

23. Violent Offenses. This is a count of the number of violent offenses included in "Arrest History." Sixteen actives (1.0 percent) and one inactive had one such arrest; none had more than one. None of these arrests resulted in a conviction. Four blacks with a history of an arrest for a violent crime were admitted in 1957.

24. Summonses. This is the number of items listed by the subject on his application in response to the instruction, "Indicate below every summons or subpoena received in other than a civil action." Most of the items involved traffic violations or automobile accidents. The average number of summonses listed was 1.2. No significant differences were found by race or active/inactive status.

25. Court Appearances. This is a count of the entries under the instruction, "Indicate every civil action or proceeding in which you were summoned or subpoenaed or in which you were a party." If the subject listed incidents in which he was a witness but the case never came to court, these were not counted. Twelve percent of the applicants recorded one or more such incidents; no significant difference was observed by race or active/inactive status.

Investigator's Appraisal

26. Background Rating. This variable summarizes the findings of the Police Department's background investigator, a specially-trained higher ranking officer who has access to all the relevant records of the applicant and who conducts interviews with friends, neighbors, and employers as well as with the applicant himself. Aside from the rating "disapproval," which is a formal recommendation by the investigator that the applicant not be appointed, the ratings for this variable were obtained by interpreting the meaning of the investigator's report. The values for the variable Background Rating are as follows:

0 – Disapproval, Poor, or Questionable
1 – Fair
2 – Good
3 – Excellent.

Although most applicants who received a rating of "disapproval" were not appointed to the force and therefore are not members of our study cohort, the cohort does contain a few such men, since rejected applicants could appeal the decision. The distribution of this variable is shown in Table 3-12. The blacks were rated less satisfactory than the whites, significant at the .02 level by chi-square test, and the inactives were less likely to be rated very low than the actives, significant at the .005 level.

27. Negative Background. This is a nominal variable describing any characteristic the background investigator mentioned as negative. If more than one such characteristic was listed, the most serious one was coded. The frequency with which particular characteristics were mentioned is shown in Table 3-13. The men who eventually left the force had fewer instances of any negative characteristic being mentioned by the investigator.

Table 3-12
Background Investigator's Rating–Total Cohort

Background Rating	Black Actives		Total Actives		Inactives	
	Number	Percent	Number	Percent	Number	Percent
Disapproval, Poor, or Questionable	25	25.2	250	15.5	29	9.4
Fair	30	30.3	486	30.2	116	37.8
Good	41	41.4	816	50.7	155	50.5
Excellent	3	3.0	56	3.5	7	2.3
Total	99	100.0	1608	100.0	307	100.0

Distribution for black actives is significantly different from distribution for all other actives, and distribution for actives is significantly different from distribution for inactives.

Table 3-13
Negative Background—Total Cohort

Characteristics	Black Actives		White Actives		Total Actives		Inactives	
	Number	Percent	Number	Percent	Number	Percent	Number	Percent
[None mentioned]	40	40.1	760	51.2	812	50.2	219	71.3
Offenses, summonses	10	10.1	156	10.5	170	10.6	17	5.5
Disciplinary record, debts	22	22.2	327	22.0	351	21.8	45	14.7
Family probity, etc.	13	13.1	33	2.2	46	2.9	2	0.7
Medical/ psychological	4	4.0	74	5.0	79	4.9	9	2.9
Culpable omission	3	3.0	56	3.7	61	3.8	3	1.0
Other	7	7.1	78	5.3	89	5.5	12	3.9
	99	100.0	1484	100.0	1608	100.0	307	100.0

28. Recruit Score. After three months of training in the police academy, each subject took four written examinations presumably testing his understanding of the course material. A weighted average of the grades on these four exams provides the overall recruit training score. A minimum of 68 on this variable was required at the time for graduation from the academy. (At present, the passing grade is 70.) The average score for actives was 77.3, with no significant difference by race. The Recruit Score was not obtained for many inactives.

29. Unsatisfactory Probation. After graduation from the Police Training Academy, each recruit spent another six months on probation. At the end of this time, he was evaluated by his superior officer using a standard department form which is shown in Appendix B. The variable Unsatisfactory Probation is a count of all "unsatisfactory" notations on this report. About 70 percent of all subjects scored zero on this variable, with no significant differences by race or active/inactive status, as shown in Table 3-14.

30. Marksmanship. This zero-one variable records whether the officer achieved facility in handling a pistol corresponding to the Department's classification of sharpshooter, expert marksman, or marksman. Since for the most part this level is achieved early in the officer's career or not at all, the variable Marksmanship is treated as an early performance variable. Sixty-seven percent of actives scored 1 (i.e., "yes") on this variable.

Table 3-14
Probationary Evaluation—Total Cohort

Unsatisfactory Probation	Actives		Inactives	
	Number	Percent	Number	Percent
0	1092	68.7	183	73.6
1	477	30.0	64	25.4
2	21	1.3	3	1.2
3	0	–	0	–
4	1	0.0	0	–
Total	1591	100.0	252	100.0
Unknown	17		55	
Average		.33		.30

Differences are not significant.

Later Experience

31. Precinct Hazard. The Police Department rates each precinct in the City as "low," "average," "high," or "extreme" in hazard, based on its crime rate and other characteristics. These levels were scored 1, 2, 3, and 4, respectively, for the variable Precinct Hazard, which is the hazard status of the precinct in which the subject was first assigned. Most of the men (62 percent) were initially assigned to an extreme hazard precinct; practically none were assigned to low hazard precincts. The fraction of men who eventually became inactives did not vary with the hazard status of the precinct of first assignment, nor were there any differences by race on this variable. However, black officers were more likely than whites to be assigned to precincts with substantial black populations.

32. Current Residence. This is the subject's residence in 1968. By that time, only 54.1 percent of the white actives resided in the City, while 76.8 percent of the blacks did. (In 1956, at the time of application, New York City residence was required for appointment, so that all but 2 percent of the applicants resided in the City. Because of the small number of officers whose residence was outside the City at the time, it was not possible to use 1956 residence as a predictor variable.)

33. Later Education. This variable represents the level of education of the subject in 1968. The data were obtained from forms routinely distributed for update of personnel information. A subject is included in the category "some college" on this variable only if he was taking a college course during the period of time covered by the update form. For this reason, fewer subjects fell in this category in 1968 than did in 1957. See Table 3-15 for coding and distribution of this variable.

Table 3-15
Later Education—Actives

| | Black Actives | | All Actives | |
Later Education	Number	Percent	Number	Percent
1. High school equivalency diploma	16	19.5	500	32.0
2. High school graduate	47	52.3	883	56.5
3. Some college	17	20.7	108	6.9
4. Associate degree	0	–	23	1.5
5. College graduate	2	2.4	43	2.8
6. Post graduate	0	–	3	0.2
7. LLB	0	–	3	0.2
Total	82	100.0	1563	100.0
Unknown	17		45	

Summary of Characteristics of Inactives

As a whole, the men who terminated from the Department did not possess
disproportionate amounts of any characteristics that might be considered
possible indicators of future bad performance. Indeed, compared to the actives,
fewer of them were rated low by the background investigators, who as we shall
see later were successful at distinguishing good performers from bad ones.

With respect to all variables related to criminal history, employment and
military discipline, and mental disorder, the inactives were indistinguishable
from the actives. The men who leave the force tend to be younger than those
who stay and thus less likely to be married; if married, they have fewer children
and other family responsibilities. They have a greater history of occupational
mobility than those who stay on the force, and they are better educated. They
are also more likely to have military commendations. These findings are very
similar to those of Levy.[16]

In short, it appears that the New York City Police Department failed to retain
some of its best recruits in 1957. This is partially confirmed by the reasons given
by inactives for leaving the force. Nearly 38 percent joined the NYC Fire
Department, 19 percent left for other employment they considered better, 4
percent left to improve their education, and 5 percent died; this leaves only 34
percent who *may* have left for reasons related to bad performance.

Additional data available to us about inactives confirm the findings in other
departments[37] as to how long after appointment men resigned from the force.
The number of men terminating peaked in 1959, two years after appointment,
when 56 men left the Department. The annual number terminating then
decreased to 17 by 1961 and increased once again in the fifth year to 38. From
then on, the number terminating annually gradually decreased.

Correlations Among Background Variables

Simple Pearson correlation coefficients were obtained for each pair of background variables, excluding nominal variables. Those correlations that were
larger than .20 in magnitude are displayed in Tables 3-16 and 3-17 for all actives
and for black actives only. This cutoff was chosen because a correlation of .20 is
required for statistical significance at the .05 level for the black subgroup. Only
the part of the correlation matrix below the diagonal is displayed; those variables
that had no correlations larger than .20 with variables lower on the list are not
repeated in the column headings.

The following variables showed no correlations larger in magnitude than .20
with the other background variables, whether the total cohort was used, or just
the black subcohort:

1. Family Mental Disorder
2. Father's Occupation
3. Military Commendations.

Table 3-16
Background Variables: Correlations × 100   **Active Cohort—Whites**

	Age	I.Q.	Civil Service	Last occupation	Military discipline	Residences	Marital status	Children	Arrest history
Age	●								
I.Q.	−21	●							
Civil Service		37	●						
Last occupation				●					
Jobs	28								
Military record	34				*				
Military discipline					●				
Residences	43					●			
Marital status	41					48	●		
Children	43					43	57	●	
Debts	27					28	35	33	
Education				23					
Arrest history									●
Violent offenses									28
Summonses	21								
Background rating					−26				−21
Recruit score		20	28						

*Automatic correlation by definition of variable

In addition, the following variables showed no correlations larger than .20 in magnitude for the total active cohort, but did show such correlations for the black subcohort:

1. Siblings
2. Employment Discipline
3. Court Appearances
4. Unsatisfactory Probation
5. Marksmanship
6. Precinct Hazard.

Table 3-17

Background Variables: Correlations × 100   Active Cohort—Blacks

	Age	I.Q.	Civil Service	Last occupation	Jobs	Employment disciplinary record	Military record	Military discipline	Residences	Marital status	Children	Debts	Arrest history	Violent offenses	Court appearances	Recruit score
Age	•															
I.Q.	−21	•														
Civil Service		24	•													
Siblings			−30													
Last occupation				•												
Jobs					•											
Employment disciplinary record					28	•										
Military record	28				25		•									
Military discipline							*	•								
Residences	35								•							
Marital status	40	−21							37	•						
Children	38	−26							50	50	•					
Debts	27									42	28	•				
Education				29				−26								
Arrest history													•			
Violent offenses	31												43	•		
Summonses	31								23	21						
Court appearances											21	23			•	
Background rating	−23	22			−22		−25					−26	−22	−23		
Recruit score	−24	23			23	24		−37					23	27	−21	•
Unsatisfactory probation				23	21											31
Marksmanship											−23					
Precinct Hazard	−21		21									−21				

*Automatic correlation by definition of variable

Patterns of significant correlations that may be observed from the tables are that the variable Age correlates with variables in several other categories; I.Q., Civil Service Score, and Recruit Score are interrelated; the personal history variables are related to each other and (for the blacks) to Court Appearances; Arrest History and Violent Offenses are interrelated; and Background Rating is negatively related to Military Discipline, Arrest History, and (for blacks) Debts, Age, and Number of Jobs.

Performance Variables

The following are the variables used to measure the performance of the active members of the cohort.

Career Advancement

1. Career Type. After discussions with high-ranking members of the Police Department as to the meaning of the career paths found in our data, this composite variable was constructed. Each subject was classified into one category (the highest-numbered category applicable to him):

0. Patrol. No assignments other than as a patrolman in some precinct command.

1. Temporarily Special. Subject had one or more assignments to plainclothes, traffic, detective, training, etc., but he eventually returned to patrol.

2. Traffic. Subject attained a permanent appointment to the Traffic Division.

3. Special. Subject attained a permanent appointment to a special assignment other than traffic or detective. Included among special assignments are planning, administration, training, youth services, community relations, and specialized investigative units.

4. Detective Candidate. Subject was considered for an appointment to the Detective Division, but was not accepted.

5. Detective Third Grade. Subject was appointed a detective and remained a detective, but was not promoted within the Detective Division. Appointment as Detective Third Grade brings a salary intermediate between that of a patrolman and a sergeant, but it is not a civil service promotion.

6. Sergeant. Subject attained the rank of sergeant, but he had not previously been a detective and he did not subsequently (by 1971) achieve a higher promotion. The rank of sergeant is achieved through civil service procedures that include a written examination.

7. Promoted Detective. Subject was promoted within the Detective Division to the rank of Detective Second Grade or Detective First Grade. These ranks carry salaries equal to those of sergeants and lieutenants, respectively.

8. Higher Promotion. Subject achieved the civil service rank of lieutenant or captain, or he was promoted to the Detective Division and subsequently obtained a civil service promotion.

The number of men in each category, as of 1971, fourteen years after appointment, is shown in Table 3-18 for black actives and for all actives. It may be seen that blacks are disproportionately appointed to detective positions, but they are underrepresented in the Traffic Division and in positions attained by civil service promotion.

2. Awards. Eight types of official commendation are conferred by the Police Department. Listed in order of increasing prestige they are

1. Excellent Police Duty
2. Meritorious Police Duty

Table 3-18
Career Type—Active Cohort

Type	Blacks		Total Actives	
	Number	Percent	Number	Percent
Patrol	26	26.3	521	32.4
Temp. Special	23	23.2	232	14.6
Traffic	4	4.0	220	13.7
Special	6	6.1	120	7.5
Detective Candidate	5	5.1	37	2.3
Detective Third Grade	18	18.2	154	9.6
Sergeant	5	5.1	168	10.4
Promoted Detective	11	11.1	85	5.3
Higher Promotion	1	1.0	68	4.2
Total	99	100.0	1608	100.0

3. Commendation
4. Exceptional Merit
5. Honorable Mention
6. Medal for Merit
7. Police Combat Cross
8. Department Medal of Honor.

Over 90 percent of the awards to members of our cohort were for Meritorious or Excellent Police Duty. These awards are mainly bestowed for arrests; for example, an officer who makes two narcotics arrests automatically receives an award of Excellent Police Duty.

The variable awards is a count of the number of awards received by the officer in the period from 1957 to 1968. For the reasons stated above, it serves as a proxy for the number of arrests made by officers; records of arrests were not maintained in NYPD personnel files during the period under study.

The distribution of this variable is shown in Table 3-19. The differences by race are not significant.

Disciplinary Actions

Complaints of misbehavior by officers may be made by members of the public, by police officers (especially supervisors), or by other law enforcement agencies. These complaints are entered into the officer's personnel file; at the time they are first entered they represent *allegations* of misconduct. For each complaint, we determined whether a departmental trial was held and whether the complaint was substantiated. For the purposes of this study, these complaints have been counted as (negative) indicators of performance in the following variables.

Table 3-19
Awards–Active Cohort

Number of Awards	Blacks		Total Cohort	
	Number	Percent	Number	Percent
0	27	27.3	488	30.4
1	34	34.3	406	25.3
2	12	12.1	244	15.2
3	10	10.1	169	10.5
4	6	6.1	106	6.5
5+	10	10.1	192	12.0
Total	99	100.0	1605	100.0
Average	1.82		1.92	

Differences are not significant.

3. Harassment. This is a count of the number of times in the 11-year study period that a complainant has charged the subject officer with unlawfully or illegally issuing a summons or making an arrest. Typical examples of these complaints are: false arrests, illegal search and seizure, unjustifiable detention in a station house or patrol car, or illegal confiscation of arrestee's property. A total of 182 officers (11.3 percent of the cohort) had one or more harassment complaints. Among black officers, 15.1 percent had one or more such complaints. The difference is not statistically significant.

4. Departmental Charges. This is a count of the number of allegations (usually by a superior officer but sometimes by a civilian) that the officer violated the Department's regulations and procedures between 1957 and 1968. This count includes the number of harassment complaints, and in addition includes the following:

1. Procedural (e.g., improper entries on Departmental records; omitted required entry from memo book)
2. Insubordination
3. Absence (e.g., from post without permission)
4. Sick Absence when not ill
5. Moonlighting (e.g., holding another job without permission)
6. Failure to Safeguard Revolver (e.g., lost revolver; negligent use of revolver)
7. Failure to Safeguard Property (e.g., lost shield; lost summons book)
8. Inappropriate Behavior Off Duty (e.g., drunkenness; police card illegally displayed)
9. Inappropriate Behavior On Duty (e.g., smoking, sleeping, reading)
10. Failure to Perform Duty Properly (e.g., lost prisoner)
11. Moral Turpitude (e.g., complaints by wife that husband is not faithful; fathered son out of wedlock)
12. Deliberate Falsification of Report (e.g., forged book entry)
13. P.A. Violations (violation of departmental rules while training in the Police Academy).

Allegations of criminal misconduct are not included in this variable (see below).

The distribution of departmental charges is shown in Table 3-20. Black subjects had more departmental complaints than white subjects.

5. Criminal Complaints. This is a count of the number of allegations of misconduct of the following types received between 1957 and 1968:

1. Consorting with Criminals (e.g., associating with prostitutes; associating with suspected gamblers)

Table 3-20
Departmental Charges–Active Cohort

Number	Black Actives		Total Actives	
	Number	Percent	Number	Percent
0	33	33.3	892	55.5
1	33	33.3	430	26.7
2	16	16.2	157	9.8
3+	17	17.2	129	8.0
Average	1.27		0.77	

Distribution and average for black actives are significantly different from those for other actives.

2. Gratuity and Shakedown (e.g., extortion, collection of fees from peddlers, free food or other merchandise)
3. Gambling and Policy Operations (e.g., receiving payment to permit gambling and policy operations)
4. False Testimony in Court (e.g., perjury, testifying falsely regarding his actions)
5. Criminal Offenses–First 8 FBI Uniform Crime Codes (e.g., mainly larceny, burglary, and robbery)
6. Criminal Offenses–Other FBI Uniform Crime Codes (e.g., intoxication, narcotics).

A total of 134 subject officers (8.3 percent) had one or more such complaints in their files. For blacks, the corresponding figure is 9 (9.1 percent), which is not significantly different.

6. Civilian Complaints. This is the number of allegations (usually from civilians, but sometimes from other officers) processed by the Civilian Complaint Review Board in the period 1957-1968. These complaints fall into the following categories:

1. Unnecessary Force (e.g., assaults on people or suspects; brutality)
2. Abuse of Authority (e.g., harassment, threatening people, destruction of property, breaking in a door, upsetting a peddler's pushcart)
3. Discourteous Behavior (e.g., impoliteness, rude language, laughing at complainant)
4. Ethnic Slurs (e.g., religious prejudice, racial remarks).

The distribution of this variable, broken down into several categories, is shown in Table 3-21. The differences by race are not significant.

Table 3-21
Civilian Complaints—Active Cohort

| | Blacks | | Total Actives | |
Number of Civilian Complaints	Number	Percent	Number	Percent
No complaints	71	71.7	1226	76.2
One complaint, unnecessary force	14	14.1	146	9.1
One complaint, other	7	7.1	143	8.9
2+ complaints, unnecessary force	7	7.1	73	4.5
2+ complaints, other	0	—	20	1.2
Average	0.384		0.318	

Differences are not significant.

7. Total Complaints. This is the sum of all allegations of the preceding three types, including some allegations whose type was "unknown" and that were therefore not included in the above counts. The distribution of this variable is shown in Table 3-22. The larger number of complaints for blacks is accounted for by differences in departmental charges.

8. Trials. This is the total number of complaints brought to departmental trial. Thirty percent of actives had one or more charges brought to trial, while nearly 50 percent of black actives experienced a departmental trial. This corresponds to differences in Total Complaints noted above.

9. Substantiated Complaints. This variable is the count of the total number of complaints that were substantiated after departmental trial. Of the 883 men who had one or more complaints, 451 (51.1 percent) had one or more substantiated complaints. Among black officers, 50 out of 81 with complaints (61.7 percent) had at least one substantiated complaint.

As has been discussed elsewhere by Cohen,[38] only certain types of allegations are likely to be brought to trial or substantiated. The majority of civilian complaints against members of the cohort were dismissed, and only 4 percent of civilian complaints resulted in any sanction or punishment against the officer. None of the harassment complaints resulted in a departmental trial. By contrast, some 71 percent of the remaining types of departmental complaints were brought to trial, and over 78 percent of these were substantiated. Allegations of criminal misconduct would ordinarily be prosecuted in criminal courts, with a departmental trial being held when certain evidence could be presented only under the less restrictive procedures of such trials. Only 15 percent of criminal allegations were handled by departmental trial.

Table 3-22
Total Complaints—Active Cohort

	Black		White		Total Actives	
Number	Number	Percent	Number	Percent	Number	Percent
0	21	21.2	638	43.0	670	41.7
1	29	29.3	410	27.6	448	27.0
2	23	23.2	204	13.7	228	14.2
3	12	12.1	106	7.1	119	7.4
4	7	7.1	54	3.6	63	3.9
5	4	4.0	33	2.2	38	2.4
6	1	1.0	16	1.1	17	1.1
7	1	1.0	8	0.5	9	0.6
8	1	1.0	5	0.3	6	0.4
9			2	0.1	2	0.1
10			1	0.1	1	0.1
11			3	0.2	3	0.2
12			1	0.1	1	0.1
13						
14						
15						
16			1	0.1	1	0.1
Unknown			2	0.1	2	0.1
Total	99	100.0	1484	100.0	1608	100.0
Average	1.82		1.21		1.25	

Cohen also found that allegations against detectives were less likely to be brought to trial than allegations against other officers.

Absenteeism

10. Times Sick. This is a count of the number of illnesses reported for each officer during the period from 1957 to 1968, with each illness counting as one time sick, independent of how long it lasted. The distribution of this variable is shown in Table 3-23. There are no differences by race on this variable.

11. Days Sick. This is a count of the total number of days the subject reported sick between 1957 and 1968. Despite the fact that Times Sick did not vary by race, blacks were found to have significantly fewer Days Sick than whites, by a chi-square test at the .01 level. See Table 3-24.

Table 3-23
Times Sick—Active Cohort

Times Sick	Blacks		Total Actives	
	Number	Percent	Number	Percent
0- 5	38	38.8	533	33.4
6-10	25	25.5	453	28.4
11-30	31	31.6	558	35.0
31+	4	4.1	50	3.1
Total	98	100.0	1604	100.0
Average	10.0		10.3	

Differences are not significant.

Table 3-24
Days Sick—Active Cohort

Days	Blacks		Whites	
	Number	Percent	Number	Percent
0- 29	21	21.2	281	19.1
30- 59	22	22.2	302	20.5
60- 99	32	32.3	305	20.7
100-199	19	19.2	377	25.5
200+	4	4.0	205	13.9
Total	98	100.0	1470	100.0
Unknown	1		14	
Average	72.4 days		109.4 days	

Differences by race are significant.
($\chi^2 = 13.64$ with 4 d.f., $p < .01$)

Other

12. Injury Disapprovals. This is a count of the number of times an officer claimed he had been injured in the line of duty and his claim had been determined to be invalid. Somewhat under 4 percent of all subjects had one or more such incidents.

13. Firearms Removed. This is a count of the number of occasions on which an officer was requested to turn in his firearms. This would only be done in cases of grave misconduct or physical or mental disability affecting the officer's ability to handle a pistol properly. Only 27 men (1.7 percent) had their firearms removed.

14. General Performance Index. This is a composite index constructed by the authors, arrived at by weighting several individual performance measures. The index is described in detail in Chapter 5.

For Detectives Only

15. Arrest Activity. The total number of arrests made by the officer during the first six months of 1968.

This was broken down into the following two subcategories:

16. Felony Arrests. The average for this variable was 24.8.

17. Misdemeanor Arrests. The average for this variable was 14.8.

18. Evaluation. This variable is based on an evaluation report filled out by the detective's supervisor routinely twice a year. A copy of this form is given in Appendix B. The supervisor rates each officer in his command as outstanding, above average, average, unsatisfactory, or "not observed" on each of the following traits:

1. Judgment
2. Job knowledge
3. Dependability
4. Job attitude
5. Relations with people.

He then gives "a comprehensive appraisal, consistent with ratings of individual factors" The variable Evaluation was constructed from the most recent evaluation report available for each detective in 1968 by counting each "outstanding" mark as 4, each "above average" as 3, each "average" as 2, and each "unsatisfactory" as 1; the results were then averaged, ignoring factors marked "not observed." The average for this variable was 2.2.

* * *

For convenient reference in later sections of this report, the names of all the background and performance variables are displayed in Table 3-25, together with the names we have given to groupings of these variables.

**Summary of Differences in Background
Characteristics and Performance by Race**

The number of Hispanic officers in the 1957 cohort was too small to permit statistical analysis of their differences from other officers. The black subjects were found to differ significantly from whites on a small number of demo-

Table 3-25
Predictor and Performance Variables

Predictor Variables	Early Performance
1. Race	28. Recruit Score
2. Age	29. Unsatisfactory Probation
	30. Marksmanship
Mental Examinations	
3. I.Q.	Later Experience
4. Civil Service	31. Precinct Hazard
	32. Current Residence
Family Descriptors	33. Later Education
5. Family Mental Disorder	
6. Region of Birth	
7. Siblings	
8. Father's Occupation	
Occupational History	**Performance Variables**
9. Last Occupation	1. Career Type
10. Jobs	2. Awards
11. Employment Disciplinary Record	
	Disciplinary Actions
Military History	3. Harassment
12. Military Record	4. Departmental Charges
13. Military Discipline	5. Criminal Complaints
14. Military Commendations	6. Civilian Complaints
	7. Total Complaints
Personal History	8. Trials
15. Residences	9. Substantiated Complaints
16. Marital Status	
17. Children	Absenteeism
18. Debts	10. Times Sick
19. Psychological Disorder	11. Days Sick
20. Education	
	Other
Incidents Involving Police & Courts	12. Injury Disapprovals
21. Arrest History	13. Firearms Removed
22. Offense Type	14. General Performance Index
23. Violent Offenses	
24. Summonses	For Detectives Only
25. Court Appearances	15. Arrest Activity
	16. Felony Arrests
Investigator's Appraisal	17. Misdemeanor Arrests
26. Background Rating	
27. Negative Background	

graphic variables, namely Region of Birth, Marital Status, Residences, and Father's Occupation, but the only background characteristic of logical relevance for selection on which they differred from whites was their higher level of education.

Black subjects were not different from whites in regard to I.Q. or Civil Service scores, any aspect of employment or military history, or the number of incidents involving the police or courts, including Arrests, Summonses, and Court Appearances. Despite these important factors on which there were no significant differences by race, the black subjects were rated lower than white subjects by the Police Department's background investigators.

After appointment, the black officers were rated the same as white officers on Recruit Score and Unsatisfactory Probation, and they had the same numbers of Civilian Complaints, allegations of Harrassment, and Criminal Complaints. However, they accumulated, on the average, 65 percent more Departmental Charges than white officers.

The black officers did not progress through civil service ranks as well as white officers, but they were disproportionately over-represented in the detective ranks. Since detectives' salaries are comparable to those of sergeants and lieutenants, the average current salary of black officers appointed in 1957 is about the same as the average for white officers, or perhaps slightly higher. The fraction of black officers who terminated their employment with the Police Department was also the same as the fraction of whites.

4

Relationships of Predictor Variables with Performance

In this chapter, we will describe the patterns of the relationships of the predictor variables with the performance variables. For the most part, these observations were drawn from pairwise cross-tabulation of the variables; however, in some cases we also summarize the findings from the regression analysis, which is presented in greater detail in Chapter 5. In each instance, we first describe the relationships found for the entire active cohort, and then we mention whatever differences were found for the black subcohort taken separately. Unless we specifically state otherwise, all patterns reported here attained a statistical significance of .05 by chi-square test.[a] In some cases, we employ a complementary test of significance, namely that the contribution of the predictor to reducing the variance of the performance measure, when entered into the appropriate regression equation, had to be significantly different from zero at the .05 level by F test.

The following predictor variables were found to have no significant relationships with any of the performance variables, and therefore will not be discussed further:

1. Father's Occupation
2. Family Mental Disorder
3. Residences
4. Children.

In addition, the performance data collected specifically for detectives were not significantly associated with any of the background variables. The discussion below covers the relationship of each of the remaining predictor variables with the first thirteen performance measures shown on Table 3-25.

Age vs. Performance

The age of the subject at the time of appointment was found to be related in important ways to Career Type, Disciplinary Actions, and Absenteeism, but not to Awards or other performance variables.

---

[a]Because several hundred cross-tabulations were inspected, it is important to note that in 100 cross-tabulations of unrelated variables, 5 tables would be expected to pass this test by chance alone. We therefore report the actual level of significance, which in many cases is considerably smaller than .05.

Age vs. Career Type

The cross-tabulation of Age against Career Type is shown in Table 4-1. The men who were oldest at time of appointment were much less likely to advance beyond a patrol assignment than the younger men; when they did advance, they were more likely to do so through the detective route than through civil service appointments. Thus, for example, 18.8 percent of the men who were 21-24 years old at the time of appointment obtained civil service promotions within 14 years, but only 4.2 percent of those aged 30 or over did so. Looking at the detective positions, we see that a somewhat higher proportion of the older men than younger men became detectives; among those who did obtain such positions, over half of the older men were promoted within the Detective Division, while less than a third of the youngest men were so promoted.

Another interesting finding is that about the same proportions of men of all ages were given special assignments, but the oldest men were more likely to remain in their special assignments rather than return to patrol. This may be related to the fact that a substantial number of the younger men currently in special assignments could have been counted in the categories of Sergeant and Higher Promotion for the variable Career Type.

When the predictor variables were entered into a regression equation for Career Type, Age was found to be the third most important predictor, after Recruit Score and Civil Service.

Age vs. Disciplinary Actions

The subjects who were youngest at the time of appointment accumulated slightly more Total Complaints than the older men, but a smaller proportion of them were substantiated by departmental trial, so that there are no significant relationships between Age and Substantiated Complaints.

As shown in Table 4-2, the main contributor to the observed difference was Civilian Complaints; there were no significant differences by age for Departmental Charges, Criminal Complaints, or Harassment. We found that 24.9 percent of the officers aged 21-24 at time of appointment had at least one civilian complaint, compared to only 16.7 percent of the men aged 30 or more. Moreover, these additional complaints against the younger officers involved charges of use of unnecessary force: 15 percent of the men aged 21 to 24 at appointment received allegations of unnecessary force, compared to only 7 percent of the over 30 group. There were no similar differences for allegations of abuse of authority, discourteous behavior, or ethnic slurs.

Considering the fact that a larger proportion of the older men than the younger men had nonsupervisory field assignments (patrol or detective), the data clearly indicate that men who are over 30 at time of appointment are less likely

53

Table 4-1

Age vs. Career Type: Total Active Cohort

													Career Type									
	Patrol		Temporarily Special		Traffic		Special		Detective Candidate		Detective Third Grade		Sergeant		Promoted Detective		Higher Promotion		Total	
Age	N	%	N	%	N	%	N	%	N	%	N	%	N	%	N	%	N	%	N	%
18-24	201	27.1	114	15.7	100	13.8	45	6.7	19	2.6	76	10.5	97	13.4	35	4.8	39	5.4	726	100.0
25-29	250	35.0	105	14.7	98	13.7	55	7.7	16	2.2	64	9.0	67	9.4	33	4.6	26	3.6	714	100.0
30+	70	41.7	16	9.5	22	13.1	20	11.9	2	1.2	14	8.3	4	2.4	17	10.1	3	1.8	168	100.0
Total	521	32.4	235	14.6	220	13.7	120	7.5	37	2.3	154	9.6	118	10.4	85	5.3	68	4.2	1608	100.0

$\chi^2 = 53.638$ with 16 d.f., $p < .001$

Table 4-2
Age vs. Civilian Complaints: Total Active Cohort

Age	None		Unnecessary Force		Abuse of Authority Discourtesy, Ethnic Slurs		Total	
	Number	Percent	Number	Percent	Number	Percent	Number	Percent
21-24	545	75.1	107	14.7	74	10.2	726	100.0
25-29	541	75.8	100	14.0	73	10.2	714	100.0
30+	140	83.3	12	7.2	16	9.5	168	100.0
Total	1226	76.2	219	13.6	163	10.1	1608	100.0

Civilian Complaints

to incur complaints based on their interactions with civilian members of the community.

Age vs. Absenteeism

The statistics show that absences for illness were substantially less common among the subjects who were older than average at time of appointment. The proportion of men for whom the number of Times Sick was under five was 40 percent for the men over 30, 35 percent for the men aged 25-29, and 30 percent for men under 25. When Age was entered into the regression equation for Times Sick, it was found to be the second most powerful predictor, after Recruit Score.

Age vs. Performance: Black Subcohort

There were no significant relationships between Age and any of the performance measures for black officers. This may be a simple mathematical consequence of the smaller sample size for blacks, since the patterns for blacks were also not significantly different from the patterns for the total cohort.

I.Q. vs. Performance

I.Q. was found to be related to certain aspects of Career Type and to Awards, but *not to other performance variables*, for the total cohort. For the black subcohort, I.Q. was found to be related to Disciplinary Actions and Absenteeism, but not to Career Type or Awards.

I.Q. vs. Career Type

As would be expected, the ranks attained by civil service promotion were predominantly occupied by men with above-average I.Q. In fact, the proportion of subjects who were sergeants, lieutenants, or captains by 1971 increased monotonically with I.Q., reaching 35.8 percent of the men with I.Q. of 120 or higher. However, it is interesting to note that 6 out of 389 subjects with I.Q. in the range 90-99 (1.5 percent of such officers) were able to attain promotions to levels higher than sergeant. See Table 4-3. In this table, and in some of those that follow, the numbers of subjects in the various categories do not add to a total of 1608. This indicates that data were missing for some subjects on one or both of the variables in the tabulation.

On the other hand, appointment to the Detective Division and promotion within detective ranks were not significantly related to I.Q. In each I.Q. range above 90, about 14 percent of the subjects were detectives in 1971, and about one-third of them were promoted.

Men who were appointed to the Traffic Division and remained there as patrolmen were predominantly of below-average I.Q. Indeed, the proportion of men in each I.Q. range who remained in the Traffic Division decreased monotonically with I.Q., from 28.6 percent of those with I.Q.s below 90 to 7.4 percent of those with I.Q. 120 or higher.

I.Q. vs. Awards

The relationship between I.Q. and Awards was not statistically significant in the cross-tabulations, but in the regression analysis, after two other variables were controlled for, higher I.Q. was found to be related to a higher number of Awards. For men with I.Q. under 90, the average number of awards was 1.36; for men in the range 90-99, the average was 1.59; for all men with higher I.Q., the average was 1.80.

I.Q. vs. Performance: Black Subcohort

The relationship between I.Q. and performance for blacks was the reverse of what one would tend to expect for all three performance measures that proved to be significantly related to I.Q.

I.Q. vs. Disciplinary Actions

The black officers with high I.Q. were significantly more likely to have received charges that resulted in a departmental trial than were officers of lower I.Q. In

Table 4-3
I.Q. vs. Career Type: Total Active Cohort

										Career Type										
I.Q.	Patrol		Temporarily Special		Traffic		Special		Detective Candidate		Detective Third Grade		Sergeant		Promoted Detective		Higher Promotion		Total	
	N	%	N	%	N	%	N	%	N	%	N	%	N	%	N	%	N	%	N	%
<90	20	40.8	5	10.2	14	28.6	6	12.2	–	–	3	6.1	1	2.0	–	–	–	–	49	100.0
90-99	139	35.7	59	15.2	67	17.2	32	8.2	14	3.6	34	8.7	16	4.1	22	5.7	6	1.5	389	100.0
100-109	245	33.8	101	13.9	100	13.8	52	7.2	16	2.2	77	10.6	71	9.8	41	5.7	22	3.0	725	100.0
110-119	97	29.6	52	15.9	29	8.8	21	6.4	6	1.8	31	9.5	57	17.4	15	4.6	20	6.1	328	100.0
120+	11	13.6	14	17.3	6	7.4	9	11.1	1	1.2	6	7.4	14	17.3	5	6.2	15	18.5	81	100.0
Total	512	32.6	231	14.7	216	13.7	120	7.6	37	2.4	151	9.6	159	10.1	83	5.3	63	4.0	1572	100.0

fact, 62 percent of black officers with I.Q. of 110 or higher had one or more Trials, as did 59 percent of those in the I.Q. range 100-109, but only 26 percent of those with I.Q. under 100 had one or more Trials. When I.Q. was entered into the regression equation for Trials, it was found to be a significant contributor to variance reduction, second only to Siblings.

This pattern was not observed to be consistent for all types of Disciplinary Actions. For example, the relationship between I.Q. and Civilian Complaints was statistically significant, and the patterns suggested that black officers with lower I.Q.s might be more likely to be subject to such allegations. In fact, 37.9 percent of black subjects with I.Q.s in the range 90-99 had at least one civilian complaint, while only 26.3 percent of those in the range 110-119 did. See Table 4-4.

I.Q. vs. Awards

The relationship between I.Q. and Awards for blacks was not statistically significant. However, the cross-tabulation (Table 4-5) shows that the pattern for blacks was not consistent with that found for whites, in which higher I.Q. was related to more awards.

I.Q. vs. Times Sick

The blacks with high I.Q. were found to be absent due to illness more frequently than other black officers. Table 4-6 shows that 25.8 percent of black officers with I.Q. under 100 were sick 11 or more times in 11 years, compared to 61.9 percent of those with I.Q. of 110 or more.

Education vs. Performance

The educational level of the subject at the time of appointment was found to be significantly related to Career Type and Disciplinary Actions, but not to Awards or other performance measures. Among the black subjects, Education did not appear to be related to any aspects of performance.

Education vs. Career Type

The data showing the relationship between Education and Career Type are presented in Table 4-7. Subjects with at least one year of college education were more likely to be promoted to sergeant, lieutenant, and captain than officers

Table 4-4
I.Q. vs. Civilian Complaints: Black Actives

I.Q.	None		Civilian Complaints						Total	
			1 Complaint of Abuse of Authority, Discourtesy or Ethnic Slurs		1 Complaint of Unnecessary Use of Force		2 Complaints of Abuse of Authority, Discourtesy or Ethnic Slurs			
	Number	Percent	Number	Percent	Number	Percent	Number	Percent	Number	Percent
<90	–	–	1	50.0	–	–	1	50.0	2	100.0
90-99	18	62.1	4	13.8	4	13.8	3	10.3	29	100.0
100-109	35	79.5	2	4.5	4	9.1	3	6.8	44	100.0
110-119	14	73.7	–	–	5	26.3	–	–	19	100.0
120+	2	100.0	–	–	–	–	–	–	2	100.0
Total	69	71.9	7	7.3	13	13.5	7	7.3	96	100.0

Table 4-5
I.Q. vs. Awards: Black Actives

I.Q.	Awards								Average
	No Awards		1 Award		2+ Awards		Total		
	Number	Percent	Number	Percent	Number	Percent	Number	Percent	
<100	7	24.1	9	31.0	13	44.8	29	100.0	1.2
100-109	12	27.3	14	31.8	18	40.9	44	100.0	1.1
110+	8	38.1	9	42.9	4	19.0	21	100.0	0.8
Total	27	28.9	32	34.0	35	37.2	94	100.0	1.1

χ^2 is not significant at .05 level.

Table 4-6
I.Q. vs. Times Sick: Black Actives

I.Q.	Times Sick					
	0-10		11+		Total	
	Number	Percent	Number	Percent	Number	Percent
<100	23	74.2	8	25.8	31	100.0
100-109	30	68.2	14	31.8	44	100.0
110+	8	38.1	13	61.9	21	100.0
Total	61	63.5	35	36.5	96	100.0

$\chi^2 = 7.80$ with 2 d.f., $p < .05$

with no college education. We found, for example, that 22.8 percent of the subjects with some college were sergeants or higher 14 years later, compared to 10.4 percent of the subjects with a high school equivalency diploma and 13.7 percent of the high school graduates. There was virtually no relationship between education and appointment to, or promotion within, the Detective Division. For example, 13.4 percent of the subjects with some college were appointed to the Detective Division, compared to 14.8 percent of the holders of high school diplomas.

Education vs. Disciplinary Actions

Subjects with some college were significantly less likely to receive civilian complaints than officers with less education. The statistics show, for example, that 12.0 percent of the subjects with some college had at least one complaint of

Table 4-7
Education vs. Career Type: Total Active Cohort

Entering Education	Patrol		Temporarily Special		Traffic		Special		Detective Candidate		Detective Third Grade		Sergeant		Promoted Detective		Higher Promotion		Total	
	N	%	N	%	N	%	N	%	N	%	N	%	N	%	N	%	N	%	N	%
Less Than High School	20	26.3	18	23.7	9	11.8	6	7.9	–	–	8	10.5	7	9.2	7	9.2	1	1.3	76	100.0
High School Equivalency Diploma	158	39.3	50	12.4	67	16.7	18	4.5	9	2.2	36	9.0	35	8.7	22	5.5	7	1.7	402	100.0
High School Graduate	258	33.7	112	14.6	103	13.5	56	7.3	16	2.1	73	9.5	75	9.8	42	5.5	30	3.9	765	100.0
Some College	77	22.8	52	15.4	40	11.9	35	10.4	11	3.3	32	9.5	49	14.5	13	3.9	28	8.3	337	100.0
Associate Degree	4	33.3	2	16.7	1	8.3	2	16.7	–	–	2	16.7	1	8.3	–	–	–	–	12	100.0
College Graduate	4	25.0	1	6.3	–	–	3	18.8	1	6.3	3	18.8	1	6.3	1	6.3	2	12.5	16	100.0
Total	521	32.4	235	14.6	220	13.7	120	7.5	37	2.3	154	9.6	168	10.4	85	5.3	68	4.2	1608	100.0

Career Type

unnecessary force, compared to 17.7 percent of the subjects with a high school equivalency diploma (see Table 4-8). When Education was introduced into the regression equation for Civilian Complaints, it emerged as the most powerful predictor of civilian complaints. There were no statistically significant relationships between Education and forms of misconduct other than Civilian Complaints, although subjects with some college tended to have fewer allegations of harassment than average.

Later Education vs. Performance

In addition to considering entering education as a predictor variable, we examined cross-tabulations between highest educational attainment of the subjects as of 1968 and the various performance measures. Although Later Education cannot be viewed as a predictor variable, its interaction with performance is of great interest. Our discussion stresses differences between college graduates and non-college graduates because most large police departments have considered the possibility of requiring a college diploma.

Later Education was found to be related inversely to Total Complaints, Trials, Substantiated Complaints, Departmental Charges, Civilian Complaints, Times Sick, and Injury Disapprovals. It was also related to Career Type, but not significantly to Criminal Complaints, Harassment, or Awards.

Later Education vs. Career Type

The data showing the relationships between Later Education and Career Type are presented in detail in Table 4-9. They show that officers who completed their college education before or during their service as policemen tended to advance much more rapidly than their less educated counterparts, especially through the civil service route. We found, for example, that 57.1 percent of the college graduates were promoted to sergeant, lieutenant, or captain, compared to 22.2 percent of the officers with some college and 12.0 percent of the high school graduates. Of the six subjects who attended graduate school or received law degrees, five were promoted to the ranks of sergeant or higher, and one was promoted within the Detective Division.

Although more than half of the college graduates advanced through civil service to the rank of sergeant or higher, only 7.0 percent held the rank of detective third-grade. This compared to 15.7 percent of the officers who were still attending college and 7.7 percent of the men who only graduated high school.

Other interesting differences between college and non-college graduates were as follows. Only 9.3 percent of the college graduates were still assigned to patrol,

Table 4-8
Education vs. Civilian Complaints: Total Active Cohort

Education	Civilian Complaints											
	None		1 Allegation of Abuse, Discourtesy or Ethnic Slurs		1 Allegation of Unnecessary Force		2+ Allegations of Abuse, Discourtesy or Ethnic Slurs		2+ Allegations With at Least 1 Unnecessary Force		Total	
	Number	Percent	Number	Percent	Number	Percent	Number	Percent	Number	Percent	Number	Percent
Less than high school	53	69.7	6	7.9	11	14.5	1	1.3	1	1.3	76	100.0
High School Equivalency Diploma	293	72.9	29	7.2	47	11.7	9	2.2	24	6.0	402	100.0
High School graduate	592	77.4	75	9.8	54	7.1	10	1.3	34	4.4	765	100.0
College	288	78.9	33	9.1	34	9.3	–	–	10	2.7	365	100.0
Total	1,226	76.2	143	8.9	146	9.1	20	1.2	73	4.5	1,608	100.0

Table 4-9
Later Education vs. Career Type: Total Active Cohort

Highest Educational Attainment	Career Type																			
	Patrol		Temporarily Special		Traffic		Special		Detective Candidate		Detective Third Grade		Sergeant		Promoted Detective		Higher Promotion		Total	
	N	%	N	%	N	%	N	%	N	%	N	%	N	%	N	%	N	%	N	%
High School Equivalency	197	39.4	69	13.8	80	16.0	26	5.2	11	2.2	40	8.0	41	8.2	28	5.6	8	1.6	500	100.0
High School Graduate	290	32.8	133	15.1	124	14.0	68	7.7	22	2.5	82	9.3	86	9.7	47	5.3	31	3.5	883	100.0
Some College	17	15.7	17	15.7	11	10.7	11	10.7	4	3.7	17	15.7	15	13.9	7	6.5	9	8.3	108	100.0
Associate Degree	1	4.3	4	17.4	1	4.3	1	4.3	–	–	7	30.4	8	34.8	–	–	1	4.3	23	100.0
College Graduate	4	9.3	1	2.3	1	2.3	11	25.6	–	–	3	7.0	11	25.6	–	–	12	27.9	43	100.0
Post Graduate	–	–	–	–	–	–	–	–	–	–	–	–	–	–	1	33.3	2	66.7	3	100.0
LLB	–	–	–	–	–	–	–	–	–	–	–	–	2	66.7	–	–	1	33.3	3	100.0
Total	509	32.6	224	14.3	217	13.9	117	7.5	37	2.4	149	9.5	163	10.4	83	5.3	64	4.1	1563	100.0

and only one college graduate remained in the Traffic Division. The corresponding proportions for officers who only graduated from high school were 32.8 percent and 14 percent, respectively. Furthermore, 25.6 percent of the college graduates held special assignments compared to 7.7 percent of the men with standard high school diplomas. We might also note that there were no differences in the rates of career advancement between persons with a high school equivalency diploma and those with a standard high school diploma.

Later Education vs. Disciplinary Actions

Officers who completed college by 1968 had statistically fewer disciplinary actions, including Total Complaints, Trials, and Substantiated Complaints, than non-college-educated subjects. We found, for example, that 16.3 percent of the college graduates had allegations of misconduct brought to trial, compared to 30.4 percent of the non-college graduates (see Table 4-10).

Holders of college diplomas also had fewer departmental charges and civilian complaints than average. For example, 25.6 percent of the college graduates were alleged to have violated departmental norms compared to 41.7 percent of the non-college graduates. Similarly, we found that the proportion of non-college graduates with civilian complaints was 24.4 percent, compared to only 8.2 percent of the college graduates, or a rate of three times as high (see Table 4-11).

Later Education vs. Other Performance Measures

Not only did college graduates tend to have a lower incidence of disciplinary actions, but they also had fewer Times Sick and fewer Injury Disapprovals than non-college graduates. The statistics show that 39 percent of the non-college graduates were recorded absent from work 11 or more times in 11 years,

Table 4-10
Later Education vs. Trials: Total Active Cohort

| Later Education | Trials | | | | | |
| | None | | 1+ | | Total | |
	Number	Percent	Number	Percent	Number	Percent
Non-College Graduates	1054	69.6	460	30.4	1514	100.0
College Graduates	41	83.7	8	16.3	49	100.0
Total	1095	70.1	468	29.9	1563	100.0

$\chi^2 = 4.47, p < .05$

Table 4-11
Later Education vs. Civilian Complaints: Total Active Cohort

| Later Education | Civilian Complaints | | | | | |
| | None | | 1+ | | Total | |
	Number	Percent	Number	Percent	Number	Percent
Non-College Graduates	1145	75.6	369	24.4	1514	100.0
College Graduates	45	91.8	4	8.2	49	100.0
Total	1190	76.1	373	23.9	1563	100.0

Yates χ^2 = 6.0, $p < .05$

Table 4-12
Later Education vs. Times Sick: Total Active Cohort

| Later Education | Times Sick | | | | | |
| | 0-10 | | 11+ | | Total | |
	Number	Percent	Number	Percent	Number	Percent
Non-College Graduates	915	61.0	586	39.0	1501	100.0
College Graduates	39	81.3	9	18.7	48	100.0
Total	954	61.6	595	38.4	1549	100.0

Yates χ^2 = 7.3, $p < .01$

compared to only 18.6 percent of the college graduates, or a rate two times as high (see Table 4-12). Thus, the men who attended college while on the force were able to do so without excessive absenteeism.

Finally, we found that of the 26 subjects who had their firearms removed for cause not one had graduated college.

Region of Birth vs. Performance

For the total cohort, no significant differences were found in the performance levels of those born in New York City vs. those born elsewhere. This is probably accounted for by the small fraction of men born outside the City. Among the black subjects, a substantial portion of the total (31 out of 99 men) were born outside New York City, and our data show that they generally performed more effectively than the native New Yorker.

The strongest difference was that black subjects born outside the City advanced more rapidly in the Department than their City-born counterparts. We found that 38.8 percent of the officers born outside the City were appointed to the Detective Division, compared to 25.0 percent of the men born in the City. On the other hand, fewer officers born outside the City remained assigned to patrol (19.4 percent) compared to officers born in the City (29.4 percent). When Region of Birth for black subjects was introduced into the regression equation for Career Type, it attained statistical significance at the .05 level and emerged as the second most powerful explanatory factor next to Recruit Score. The addition of Region of Birth into the regression equation increased the multiple correlation coefficient from .253 to .341, thereby accounting for an additional 5.2 percent of the variation.

In addition to career advancement, a black officer's place of birth appeared to be slightly associated with indices of misconduct, although these relationships did not attain statistical significance. The general direction of these relationships was that the men born outside the City had less misconduct. For example, 83.8 percent of the native New Yorkers had one or more Total Complaints, compared to 67.7 percent of those born outside the City. Most of the difference was accounted for by Departmental Complaints.

Siblings vs. Performance

The number of siblings in an officer's family was unrelated to police perform-ance for the white subjects, but there was one significant association for the blacks. We found that the black officers with no siblings had a higher incidence of Trials and Substantiated Complaints than any other group. When Siblings entered the regression equation for Trials, it emerged as the most powerful predictor, producing a correlation coefficient of .254 which was significant at the .05 level.

Occupational History vs. Performance

Neither the number of jobs held by subjects prior to application nor the type of work performed at the most recent job was related in any important way to any of the later performance variables, except that a high ranking on Last Occupa-tion was associated with later promotion within the Police Department. For example, nearly 38.3 percent of officers whose Last Occupation rated above 50 received civil service promotions or appointments to the Detective Division, compared to 28.4 percent of those under 50. Although it might be thought that this relationship would be accounted for by the differences in age and intelligence of the men in high-rated occupations, in fact it was found that even when such variables were accounted for in a regression equation for Career Type, a significant contribution was still made by Last Occupation. Despite the presence of statistical significance, the relationship was not so strong as to be of great practical interest.

On the other hand, a history of employment disciplinary actions was found to be strongly related to later disciplinary actions as a police officer. The most striking relationship was between Employment Discipline and Substantiated Complaints. The statistics show that 39 percent of the men with an employment disciplinary record had at least one substantiated complaint, compared to 26.5 percent of the subjects without a derogatory employment record. Employment Discipline emerged as the fourth most powerful predictor, after Unsatisfactory Probation, Recruit Score, and Military Discipline, when entered into the regression equation for Substantiated Complaints, attaining statistical significance at the .001 level.

The higher incidence of misconduct for subjects with a prior employment disciplinary record was a result of a higher rate of alleged violations of departmental norms (see Table 4-13). We found that 53.7 percent of the subjects with several employment disciplinary actions had recorded instances of departmental violations compared to 43.4 percent of the subjects without any. The relationship between Employment Discipline and Departmental Charges attained statistical significance in the regression equation ($p < .001$) and produced a multiple correlation coefficient of .216 together with three other factors— Unsatisfactory Probation, Background Rating, and Recruit Score.

The relationships were similar for the black subjects, although statistical significance was not obtained in the regression equations. We found, for example, that 53.9 percent of the black officers with a past record of employment disciplinary actions had at least three allegations of misconduct, compared to 22.3 percent of the other officers, a proportion nearly two and a half times as high. The higher rate of misconduct was primarily a result of departmental complaints and complaints of harassment. We found that the percentages of black subjects with a prior disciplinary record who scored one or more on Departmental Charges and Harassment were 78.6 and 28.6, respectively. The corresponding proportions were 64.7 percent and 13 percent for officers without past employment misconduct.

Employment Discipline was not found to be related to positive measures of police performance, such as Awards and Career Type. There was some indication that subjects with an employment disciplinary record were absent more frequently than others, but the differences were not large.

Military History vs. Performance

In general, the officers who had served in the military performed no better or worse than those who had no military service. There was a slight indication that veterans tended to obtain a larger number of awards than other officers, but this

Table 4-13
Employment Discipline vs. Departmental Complaints: Total Active Cohort

Employment Discipline	Departmental Charges									
	None		1		2		3+		Total	
	Number	Percent	Number	Percent	Number	Percent	Number	Percent	Number	Percent
None	799	56.6	378	26.8	134	9.5	100	7.1	1411	100.0
1	73	47.4	39	25.3	19	12.3	23	14.9	154	100.0
2+	19	46.3	13	31.7	4	9.8	5	12.2	41	100.0
Total	891	55.5	430	26.8	157	9.8	128	8.0	1606	100.0

$\chi^2 = 16.1$ with 6 d.f., $p < .02$

relationship did not appear in direct cross-tabulations of Military Record vs. Awards; it could only be detected through regression analysis after three other variables were controlled. (See Chapter 5.) In terms of career advancement, disciplinary actions, absenteeism, and other performance variables, no significant differences were found between veterans and non-veterans.

In addition, the presence of military commendations in a candidate's record was not found to be a meaningful predictor of later performance. It is particularly interesting to note that Military Commendations was not even significantly related to the performance variable Awards, which might be expected to increase with the number of military commendations. Thus, we do not find any indication that good performance in the military is related to later good performance as a police officer.

However, a very strong relationship was found between bad performance in the military (as measured by the variable Military Discipline) and later bad performance as a policeman. Evidence of later bad performance appeared for several types of disciplinary actions, as will be described below, but not in lessened performance as measured by Awards or Career Type. The patterns were similar for both black and white officers, although the relationships were found to be stronger for the whites. In all these respects, the predictor Military Discipline is very similar to the predictor Employment Discipline.

Military Discipline vs. Later
Disciplinary Actions: Total Cohort

An increasing number of recorded military disciplinary actions was associated with an increasing number of Total Complaints, Trials, and Substantiated Complaints. We found, for example, that 65.5 percent of the officers with a record of several military disciplinary actions (more than one) had been alleged to have engaged in some form of police misconduct, compared to 57.2 percent of the subjects without a military disciplinary record (see Table 4-14). Similarly, 27.7 percent of the subjects with excessive military disciplinary actions scored higher than 2 on Total Complaints, compared to 14.4 percent of the men without a similar record. Also, 38.7 percent of the subjects with several military disciplinary actions were brought to trial for misconduct, compared to only 28.9 percent of the officers without a record, and the corresponding proportions of officers with substantiated complaints were 36.1 percent and 27.1 percent. All of the foregoing relationships attained statistical significance in the regression analysis. For example, when Military Discipline was entered into the regression equation for Substantiated Complaints, it emerged as the third strongest predictor, after Unsatisfactory Probation and Recruit Score.

Subjects with military disciplinary actions had a higher incidence of Departmental Complaints, civilian complaints involving the unnecessary use of force,

Table 4-14
Military Discipline vs. Total Complaints: For Actives Who Served in the Military

Military Discipline	Total Complaints: None		1		2		3		4+		Total	
	Number	Percent	Number	Percent	Number	Percent	Number	Percent	Number	Percent	Number	Percent
None	394	42.8	266	28.9	127	13.8	62	6.7	71	7.7	920	100.0
1	113	37.7	82	27.3	56	18.7	23	7.7	26	8.7	300	100.0
2+	41	34.5	33	27.7	12	10.1	15	12.6	18	15.1	119	100.0
Total	548	40.9	381	28.5	195	14.6	100	7.5	115	8.6	1339	100.0

$\chi^2 = 20.115$ with 8 d.f., $p < .001$

and complaints of Harassment. But they had a normal incidence of allegations of corruption. We found, for example, that 49.5 percent of the subjects with military disciplinary actions had been alleged to have violated departmental norms compared to 43 percent of the subjects without similar actions. Moreover, 13.4 percent of the subjects with several military disciplinary actions had at least three departmental complaints compared to only 6.8 percent of the subjects without a military disciplinary record. We also found that 20.1 percent of the subjects possessing a military disciplinary record were alleged to have used unnecessary force compared to 13 percent of the subjects without a prior military disciplinary record. There were no differences among the subjects regardless of past military experience in other types of civilian complaints such as abuse of authority, ethnic slurs, and discourteous behavior. Likewise, the proportions of complaints characterizable as corruption were nearly equal for all subjects regardless of prior military record.

Military Discipline vs. Later Disciplinary
Actions: Black Subcohort

Among black officers, the presence of a military disciplinary record was also found to be related to Total Complaints, Trials, and Substantiated Complaints, although these relationships were not statistically significant in the regression equations as they were for the white officers.

Our data showed, for example, that 56.9 percent of the black officers without a past record of military misconduct had substantiated complaints compared to 39.0 percent of the other black officers. The difference was due mainly to Departmental Charges and Civilian Complaints. We found that 69 percent of the men without a military disciplinary record were alleged to have engaged in departmental misconduct compared to 60.9 percent of the officers with a disciplinary record. Although the differences in the incidence of civilian complaints among black officers with varying military disciplinary backgrounds were small, the differences in the number of allegations involving the unnecessary use of force were substantial. The data in Table 4-15 show that exactly a third of the men with military disciplinary records were alleged to have used unjustified force, compared to 16.0 percent of the men without a similar record, or a proportion about twice as high.

Marital Status vs. Performance

No relationships between a subject's marital status at time of appointment and his later performance were found to be significant. Nonetheless, the general patterns were about what one would expect, given the relationship between age

Table 4-15
Military Discipline vs. Civilian Complaints: Black Actives

	Civilian Complaints									
Military Discipline	No Complaints		1 Complaint of Abuse of Authority Discourtesy, Ethnic Slurs		1 Complaint of Unnecessary Force		2 Complaints; One Unnecessary Force		Total	
	Number	Percent	Number	Percent	Number	Percent	Number	Percent	Number	Percent
None	42	72.4	5	8.6	5	8.6	6	10.3	58	100.0
1	16	69.6	0	–	6	26.1	1	4.3	23	100.0
2+	4	57.6	0	–	3	42.9	0	–	7	100.0
Total	62	70.5	5	5.7	14	15.9	7	8.0	88	100.0

and performance and the fact that the older men were more likely to be married. Thus, for example, the married men were somewhat more likely to become detectives later, and they had slightly fewer disciplinary actions.

Debts vs. Performance

Although the number of debts outstanding against an applicant did not emerge as a significant predictor of any of the individual measures of his later performance, the patterns revealed by all the performance variables taken together suggest that men with a large number of debts (three or more) are somewhat less satisfactory performers than average. For example, while 26.3 percent of men with no debts were found to have one or more substantiated complaints 11 years later, and 28.6 percent of men with one debt had substantiated complaints, the corresponding figure for men with three or more debts was 38.4 percent. The difference was not an indicator of a greater number of corruption charges against men with many debts, but arose from a larger number of departmental complaints.

These men with many debts also had a higher than average frequency of Injury Disapprovals and a larger number of Times Sick. The only countervailing pattern seen for these men was that they appeared to have slightly more Awards than men without debts: 78.0 percent of the subjects who reported three or more debts had awards, compared to 68.2 percent of those with no debts. For the black subcohort, no consistent patterns were found between Debts and Performance variables. Again, no significant relationships were found, and the black subjects with many debts were somewhat better than average on some performance measures, somewhat worse on others.

Arrest History vs. Performance

An extremely interesting difference was found between the officers who had been arrested prior to joining the force and those who had not. The difference occurred for the variable Harassment, which measures the number of times an officer is accused by a civilian of making a false or illegal arrest or of detaining a person without cause. Those officers who had themselves been arrested at one time scored significantly *lower* on this variable than other officers, which means they were more careful about the rights of arrested persons. The data showed that only 4.4 percent of men with one or more prior arrests had allegations of Harassment in their records, while on the average 12 percent of officers had such allegations. When Arrest History was entered into the regression equation for Harassment, it emerged as the second of two statistically significant factors, after Court Appearances.

Arrest History was not found to be significntly related to any other performance variables, and in particular there was no association between an early arrest history and later allegations of corruption or departmental misconduct. Thus, the men who succeed in getting appointed to the Police Department despite an arrest history appear to perform at least as well as those without prior arrests.

In the case of black officers, there were only 11 men with a prior arrest history, so that no significant patterns emerged. However, if anything, these men seemed to be good performers: 3 of them were promoted to sergeant or lieutenant, and on the average they had more awards and fewer disciplinary actions than men without arrest histories.

Another small subgroup that bears closer inspection consists of the 16 men who had previously been arrested for a crime of violence. Again, no significant relationships were found, but these men appeared to be poor performers on practically every variable. Seventy-five percent of them had one or more complaints of misconduct (compared to 58.3 percent on average), 43.7 percent of them had one or more civilian complaints (compared to 23.8 percent), and two of the sixteen men were alleged to have engaged in corruption. These men also won fewer awards than average. Such findings, though not conclusive, suggest the importance of studying a larger sample of police officers with a prior history of arrest for violent crimes to determine their performance patterns.

Psychological Disorder vs. Performance

Since only 29 out of the 1608 members of the active cohort had a previous history of psychological disorder, the sample size was too small to produce statistically significant relationships between Psychological Disorder and any of the performance variables. However, the data suggest that men with previous psychological disorders achieve promoted positions as frequently as other men, but they have a somewhat higher incidence of departmental complaints and absenteeism than average.

Summonses vs. Performance

Several statistically significant relationships were found between the number of court summonses reported by an applicant and later misconduct as a police officer, but these were not monotonic. Instead, the men who reported one summons appeared to be less likely to engage in misconduct than either those who reported none or those who reported more than one summons.

For example, we see on Table 4-16, which shows Summonses vs. Trials, that men who had one summons had significntly fewer complaints brought to trial

Table 4-16
Summonses vs. Trials: Total Active Cohort

	Trials										
	None		1		2		3		4+		Total	
Summonses	Number	Percent	Number	Percent	Number	Percent	Number	Percent	Number	Percent	Number	Percent
0	535	71.9	135	18.1	40	5.4	18	2.4	16	2.2	744	100.0
1	243	73.6	64	19.4	13	3.9	5	1.5	5	1.5	330	100.0
2+	344	64.8	137	25.8	35	6.6	5	.9	10	1.9	531	100.0
Total	1,122	69.9	336	20.9	88	5.5	28	1.7	31	1.9	1,605	100.0

$\chi^2 = 19.4$ with 8 d.f., $p < .02$

Table 4-17
Summonses vs. Substantiated Complaints: Total Active Cohort

	Substantiated Complaints							
	No Charges		Unsubstantiated Complaints		Substantiated Complaints		Total	
Summonses	Number	Percent	Number	Percent	Number	Percent	Number	Percent
0	323	43.3	221	29.6	202	27.1	746	100.0
1	144	43.6	111	33.6	75	22.7	330	100.0
2+	203	38.2	155	29.2	173	32.6	531	100.0
Total	670	41.7	487	30.3	450	28.0	1,607	100.0

$\chi^2 = 11.3$ with 4 d.f., $p < .03$

than other men. In fact, the men with two or more summonses had 30.6 percent more trials per man than those with one summons. This pattern persisted for Substantiated Complaints, as shown in Table 4-17, but we also see from this table that the proportions of men with no complaints whatsoever were about the same for men with no summonses and those with one summons.

In terms of the performance variable Awards, the men with the highest number of summonses appeared to be the best performers. For example, we found that 73.4 percent of the officers with several summonses (more than one) won awards, compared to 68.2 percent of the men with one summons. The differences were even greater for men who won many awards: the proportions of men with an excessive number of summonses (more than two) who won three or more awards was 33.2 percent, compared to 25.4 percent of the men without any summonses. The relationship between summonses and awards attained statistical significance in the regression analysis ($p < .05$).

For the black subcohort, no significant relations were found between Summonses and Performance variables, but the patterns observed were consistent with the hypothesis that a high number of summonses was definitely not an indicator of poor performance, and might in fact be associated with better performance than average.

Court Appearances vs. Performance

Our data show that men who are involved in civil court proceedings prior to applying for appointment to the Police Department are much more likely than others to have later allegations of mistreatment of civilians. For the total cohort, a very strong relationship was found between Court Appearances and Harassment, as shown in Table 4-18. Although only 10.5 percent of subjects without an appearance in civil court were later charged with false arrest, illegal search,

Table 4-18
Court Appearances vs. Harassment: Total Active Cohort

Court Appearances	Harassment							
	None		1		2+		Total	
	Number	Percent	Number	Percent	Number	Percent	Number	Percent
None	1259	89.5	130	9.2	18	1.3	1407	100.0
1	151	85.3	19	10.7	7	4.0	177	100.0
2+	16	66.7	7	29.2	1	4.2	24	100.0
Total	1426	88.7	156	9.7	26	1.6	1608	100.0

$\chi^2 = 19.457$ with 4 d.f., $p < .001$

etc., fully a third of the men with two or more court appearances were so charged. Court appearances was the strongest predictor in the regression equation for Harassment.

For the black subcohort a similar, although not identical, pattern was seen. In this case, it was found that officers with previous involvement in civil proceedings were more likley than average to have Civilian Complaints, especially of the use of unnecessary force (see Table 4-19). This relationship also attained statistical significance in the regression analysis. These findings provide some indication that officers with a history of court appearances may have difficulty in interacting with citizens.

Factors Pertaining to the Recruitment Process

There are four major factors that reflect the process of application and recruitment to the New York City Police Department. They include Civil Service, Background Rating, Recruit Score, and Unsatisfactory Probation. A brief description of these factors in relationship to the recruitment process will be useful in interpreting our statistical findings.

In order to be considered a candidate for the Police Department, each applicant must take and pass the Civil Service Examination for Patrolman. The examination is administered by the Department of Personnel of the City of New York. Next, applicants must pass physical and medical examinations. Although persons who fail these exams are automatically disqualified from the application process, not all who pass necessarily receive appointments. Prior to appointment, the Police Department conducts a thorough investigation into the backgrounds of each candidate to determine proof of good character. Many applicants are rejected because the background investigators discover something from their past (e.g., possession of a serious criminal record or a history of alcoholism) that raises serious doubts about the character and integrity of the candidate. In 1968, about 15 percent of the applicants who passed the exams were rejected by the background investigators. Applicants who survive the background investigation are appointed to the Police Academy, where they undergo three months of intensive study and training to prepare for police work. During this period, the recruits in 1957 took a series of four exams that tested their knowledge of what they learned in the Academy. The individual test scores for each candidate on the four examinations were combined to produce the variable we call Recruit Score. Candidates had to obtain a minimim of 68 on Recruit Score to graduate from the Police Academy in 1957.

Candidates who completed the three-month Academy training course in 1957 spent an additional six months on probation. At the end of this period, each probationary patrolman was evaluated by his immediate supervisor. Although few of the men were in fact dismissed from the force at this phase of the

Table 4-19

Court Appearances vs. Civilian Complaints: Black Actives

Court Appearances	Civilian Complaints									
	None		1 Complaint of Abuse of Authority, Discourtesy or Ethnic Slurs		1 Complaint of Unnecessary Force		2 or More Complaints		Total	
	Number	Percent	Number	Percent	Number	Percent	Number	Percent	Number	Percent
None	63	74.1	6	7.1	13	15.3	3	3.5	85	100.0
1+	8	57.1	1	7.1	1	7.1	4	28.6	14	100.0
Total	71	71.7	7	7.1	14	14.1	7	7.1	99	100.0

recruitment process (only 7 out of nearly 2000 men), we found that 30 percent of the subjects had one or more negative ratings, which we recorded in the variable Unsatisfactory Probation.

Civil Service vs. Performance

Civil service examinations for appointment and promotion of policemen and firemen have recently come under legal challenge throughout the United States. The plaintiffs in these cases charge that the civil service tests discriminate against minority group members, in violation of the Fourteenth Amendment, the Federal Civil Rights Act, or state laws.

A major precedent for these suits is the case of Griggs vs. Duke Power Company,[39] in which the U.S. Supreme Court ruled that an employer is prohibited "from requiring a high school education or passing of a standardized general intelligence test as a condition of employment in or transfer to jobs when:

(a) neither standard is shown to be significantly related to successful job performance;
(b) both requirements operate to disqualify blacks at a substantially higher rate than white applicants; and
(c) the jobs in question formerly had been filled only by white employees as part of a long-standing practice of giving preference to whites."

In its opinion on this case, the Court stated that "if an employment practice which operates to exclude Negroes cannot be shown to be related to job performance, the practice is prohibited."

Similar issues were raised in a 1971 suit against the Minneapolis Fire Department,[40] which at the time had no black, Indian, or Mexican-American employees. The Eighth Circuit Court of Appeals ruled, *inter alia*, that the written (civil service) examination for fire fighter could not be given until it had been validated by procedures commensurate with the Equal Employment Opportunity Commission Guidelines on Employment Testing. The Alabama State Police, which also had no minority group employees, was enjoined a year later from continuing its employment practices, "including . . . examination . . . , for the purpose or with the effect of discriminating . . . on the ground of race or color."[41]

In instances where an employer has not had a history of total absence of minority group employees, the legal issues are more subtle. In the case of Chance vs. Board of Education of the City of New York,[42] the District Court for the Southern District of New York ruled that statistical evidence can be used to demonstrate that "examinations and testing procedures . . . have the effect of discriminating against Black and Hispanic candidates." "However," the Court continued, "the existence of such discrimination, standing alone, would not necessarily entitle plaintiffs to relief." It is necessary to consider, in addition, "the question of whether the examinations under attack can be validated as relevant to the requirements of the positions for which they are given, i.e., whether they are 'job related.' "

The Court identified two relevant criteria for measuring test validity. The first is *content validity*, i.e., the examination must "elicit from the candidate information that is relevant to the job for which it is given." The second is *predictive validity*, which is determined "by comparing the relative examination scores of successful candidates with their later performance on the job." In the suit against the Board of Education, the Court granted preliminary relief to the plaintiffs based on the finding that "although [the Board] has taken some steps toward securing content and predictive validity . . . , [it] has not in practice achieved the goal of constructing examination procedures that are truly job related."

At the present time, the New York City Police Department is being sued by the Guardians Association, an organization of black police officers, and the Hispanic Society[43] to prevent the future administration or use of "any test as a criterion for appointment or promotion . . . which has not been . . . validated . . . as accurately measuring the merit and fitness of candidates to perform the tasks of the position for which the test is being administered." The plaintiffs claim that the existing entry-level and promotional exams are racially biased and that "there is no correlation between performance on the exams and performance on the job being tested for."

The data used by us in the present study are not suitable for testing the proposition that the civil service examination for patrolman discriminates against blacks and Hispanics, since all the subjects of this study necessarily passed the civil service exam. We plan to report later on the results of a separate study in which the civil service examination scores and races were determined for a sample of recent applicants to the New York Police Department, including applicants who failed. However, based on our 1957 cohort data, we can address the question of predictive validity by describing the relationship between civil service exam scores and later performance as a policeman.

The data on Civil Service vs. Career Type are summarized in Table 4-20. They show that high scores were consistently associated with later promotion to the ranks of sergeant, lieutenant, and captain, which are attained by passing subsequent civil service exams, but they were not associated with appointment to the Detective Division. Of the men with civil service scores above 85, 43.4 percent were promoted to sergeant, lieutenant, or captain, while the corresponding figure for men who scored below 75 was 5.7 percent. When Civil Service was entered into the regression equation for Career Type, it emerged as the second strongest predictor, after Recruit Score. The two factors together produced a multiple correlation coefficient of .290, which was significant at the .001 level.

We also see from Table 4-20 that in each scoring category the percentage of

Table 4-20
Civil Service vs. Career Type: Total Active Cohort

Civil Service Score	Career Type																		
	Patrol		Temporarily Special		Traffic		Special		Detective Candidate		Detective Third Grade		Sergeant		Promoted Detective		Higher Promotion		Total	
	N	%	N	%	N	%	N	%	N	%	N	%	N	%	N	%	N	%	N	%
Under 74.9	207	36.7	83	14.7	108	19.1	40	7.1	17	3.0	54	9.6	28	5.0	23	4.1	4	.7	564	36.8
75-79.9	198	34.0	85	14.6	74	12.7	44	7.5	10	1.7	62	10.6	57	9.8	38	6.5	15	2.6	583	38.0
80-84.9	66	25.6	42	16.3	24	9.3	25	9.7	5	1.9	25	9.7	41	15.9	13	5.0	17	6.6	258	16.8
85+	32	24.8	13	10.1	9	7.0	8	6.2	1	.8	3	2.3	28	21.7	7	5.4	28	21.7	129	8.4
Total	503	32.8	223	14.5	215	14.0	117	7.6	33	2.2	144	9.4	154	10.0	81	5.3	64	4.2	1534	100.0

$\chi^2 = 707.813$ with 24 d.f., $p < .0001$

men appointed to the Detective Division and then promoted to the ranks of Detective Second Grade or Detective First Grade was nearly equal regardless of civil service score. The only exception was for officers with the highest scores of more than 85, who were underrepresented in the Detective Division. This is balanced by their disproportionate overrepresentation as sergeants, lieutenants, and captains.

One other interesting pattern is the consistent inverse relationship between test scores and appointment to the Traffic Division. For example, nearly three times as many officers with civil service scores under 75 were assigned to the Traffic Division (19.1 percent) compared to subjects with the highest scores over 85 (7.0 percent).

All these relationships are similar to the ones found for I.Q. vs. Career Type, but Civil Service is somewhat stronger than I.Q. as a predictor of Career Type.

Aside from the patterns just noted, there were no other significant relationships of the predictor variable Civil Service with any of the other performance measures used in this study. Specifically, for the total cohort there was no association between civil service exam scores and any form of later Disciplinary Actions, Awards, Sick Time, Injury Disapprovals, or Firearms Removal.

For the black subcohort, the situation was almost identical, except that in this case not even the relationship between Civil Service and Career Type was statistically significant. This is due to the small number of promoted black officers (six men). Half of these men had civil service scores over 80, half below. The somewhat peculiar patterns that we found for I.Q. vs. Disciplinary Actions, Awards, and Time Sick for black subjects were, for the most part, not present for Civil Service vs. these performance measures. However, we did find that blacks with high civil service scores had significantly more charges of Harassment. In fact, 30 percent of blacks with Civil Service over 80 had one or more harassment charges, compared to 12 percent of those with scores under 80.

In sum, the data indicate that, within the passing range, the scores on exams for patrolmen given in the late 1950s were not predictive of any of the measures of performance available to us, except that a high score was predictive of later passing grades on civil service exams for sergeant, lieutenant, and captain. Moreover, if the relationship between initial Civil Service score and a passing grade on these later promotion examinations had been independent of race, we would have expected to find 13 of the black subjects in positions of sergeant or higher by 1971, whereas in fact there were only six.

Since 1957, changes have been made in the civil service exams in an effort to reduce any racial bias that may have been present. We therefore cannot assert that a follow-up study of recently appointed patrolmen several years from now is likely to show the same patterns as we found for the 1957 cohort.

Background Rating vs. Performance

In contrast with the findings of McAllister[18] described in Chapter 2, we found that the rating of candidates by Police Department background investigators was a good predictor of later performance. In particular, Background Rating was significantly associated with the performance variables Career Type, Disciplinary Actions, and Sick Time. But it was not related to Awards or other performance measures.

Background Rating vs. Career Type

The findings on Background Rating vs. career advancement revealed that candidates termed "excellent" by the background investigator advanced more rapidly than subjects in any other group, while those termed "poor" were the least likely to be promoted. We found, for example, that 25.0 percent of the subjects termed excellent were promoted to the ranks of sergeant, lieutenant, and captain, compared to 15.5 percent of the men termed fair and only 9.6 percent of the lowest-rated subjects. Correspondingly, more of the men termed poor (38.8 percent) remained on patrol than of those termed excellent (21.4 percent).

However, the data revealed that the relationship between background evaluations and promotion to the Detective Division was considerably weaker than for civil service promotions. In fact, 13.6 percent of the officers rated poor by the background investigators were promoted to the Detective Division, compared to 17.9 percent of those rated excellent. Moreover, a greater proportion of officers termed poor were promoted *within* the Detective Division (5.6 percent) than subjects termed excellent (3.6 percent). There were no substantial differences between subjects termed good or fair and subjects termed poor appointed to the Detective Division.

The data also showed that the proportion of men who were permanently appointed to the Traffic Division did not vary substantially with Background Rating, as it did with I.Q. and Civil Service. In fact, 19.6 percent of men termed excellent had traffic assignments, compared to 13.5 percent of all other men, which is the reverse of the pattern seen for the other two variables.

Background Rating vs. Disciplinary Actions

Subjects termed excellent by the background investigators had the lowest incidence of misconduct, while candidates termed poor had the highest. These patterns were significant and consistent for Total Complaints, Trials, and Substantiated Complaints. We found, for example, that 68 percent of the subjects termed poor had allegations of misconduct, compared to only 35.7 percent of the subjects termed excellent. See Table 4-21. Likewise, the proportions of officers with complaints brought to trial were 41.6 percent for the poorly rated candidates, and 16.1 percent for the highly appraised subjects. The figures for Substantiated Complaints were much the same. In all cases, candidates termed fair or good had a lower incidence of misconduct than men termed poor but a higher rate than subjects termed excellent.

Table 4-21
Background Rating vs. Total Complaints: Total Active Cohort

Background Rating	Total Complaints												
	None		1		2		3		4+		Total	
	Number	Percent	Number	Percent	Number	Percent	Number	Percent	Number	Percent	Number	Percent
Disapproval or Poor	80	32.0	87	34.8	33	13.2	21	8.4	29	11.6	250	100.0
Fair, or Nothing Poor	201	41.5	123	25.4	75	15.5	42	8.7	43	8.9	484	100.0
Good	353	43.3	231	28.3	116	14.2	52	6.4	64	7.8	816	100.0
Excellent	36	64.3	7	12.5	4	7.1	4	7.1	5	8.9	56	100.0
Total	670	41.7	448	27.9	228	14.2	119	7.4	141	8.8	1,606	100.0

$\chi^2 = 31.487$ with 12 d.f., $p < .002$

None of the relationships between background appraisal and the three measures of misconduct described above attained statistical significance in the regression analysis. This was because in each regression equation a more powerful predictor that entered first was highly correlated with each of the indicators of misconduct and tended to suppress the background investigation appraisal. For example, Unsatisfactory Probation, which is correlated with background appraisal, emerged as the strongest predictor of Total Complaints. In the absence of this variable, the background investigation appraisal would have emerged as the single most powerful predictor of misconduct, significant at the .05 level.

The background investigator's evaluation of each candidate's overall potential for police work was more suitable for predicting departmental allegations than allegations of corruption, civilian complaints, or harassment. Our data show that 54.8 percent of the subjects termed poor were alleged to have violated administrative rules and procedures, compared to only 25 percent of the officers termed excellent; i.e., the complaint rate among poor subjects was twice as high. Moreover, when Background Rating entered the regression equation for Departmental Charges, it emerged as the second most powerful factor after Unsatisfactory Probation, attaining statistical significance at the .001 level. The multiple correlation coefficient produced by these two factors with Department Charges was .193.

The incidence of allegations characterizable as corruption, civilian complaints, and harassment did not differ substantially regardless of the level of background appraisal. For example, approximately 5 percent each of the candidates termed poor and fair were alleged to have engaged in acts of corruption.

Background Rating vs. Times Sick

Subjects with poor background appraisals had significantly greater absenteeism than their counterparts with high ratings. The relationship is displayed in Table 4-22, which shows that 43.9 percent of poorly rated candidates were absent more than ten times, compared to only 29.1 percent of subjects rated excellent. When Background Rating was entered into the regression equation for Times Sick, it emerged as the third most powerful predictor, after Recruit Score and Age, and it attained significance at the .05 level.

Background Rating vs. Performance:
Black Subcohort

The relationships between Background Rating and performance variables for blacks were not significantly different from the patterns observed for the total cohort, except that there was no apparent association between Background

Table 4-22
Background Rating vs. Times Sick: Total Active Cohort

Background Rating	0-5		6-10		Times Sick 11-30		31+		Total	
	Number	Percent	Number	Percent	Number	Percent	Number	Percent	Number	Percent
Disapproval or Poor	80	32.3	59	23.8	96	38.7	13	5.2	248	15.6
Fair, or Nothing Poor	139	28.9	153	31.8	174	36.2	15	3.1	481	30.2
Good	289	35.7	227	28.0	274	33.8	20	2.5	810	50.8
Excellent	25	45.5	14	25.5	14	25.5	2	3.6	55	3.5
Total	533	33.4	453	28.4	558	35.0	50	3.1	1,594	100.0

$\chi^2 = 18.3$ with 9 d.f., $p < .04$

Rating and Career Type for the blacks. In any event, none of the relationships for the black subcohort attained statistical significance.

Recruit Score vs. Performance

The recruit training score turned out to be one of the most powerful and consistent predictors of later police performance. It was significantly related to Career Type, Disciplinary Actions, Sick Time, and Awards. In all respects, men with high recruit training scores were much better performers than those with low scores.

Recruit Score vs. Career Type

The statistics show that increasing recruit training scores were associated with rapid career advancement through civil service promotions, although not with appointments to the Detective Division. We found, for example, that 21.2 percent of officers with the highest recruit training scores (86-94) were sergeants, compared to 2.5 percent of the men with the lowest scores (68-70), a rate over eight times as high. Similarly, subjects with high scores advanced beyond sergeant more rapidly than average. The data show that 20.2 percent of the officers with high scores were promoted to the ranks of lieutenant and captain, compared to 0.8 percent of the men with the lowest scores, a rate 25 times as high. More rapid advancement with increasing test scores was also the pattern for subjects with intermediate scores. See Table 4-23. When Recruit Score was entered into the regression equation for Career Type, it emerged as the strongest predictor. The correlation coefficient between Recruit Score and Career Type was .241, which was statistically significant at the .001 level.

Recruit Score vs. Disciplinary Actions

Subjects with high recruit training scores had a lower than average incidence of Total Complaints, Trials, and Substantiated Complaints. As shown on Table 4-24, the proportion of subjects who had charges brought to departmental trial decreased monotonically with Recruit Score, from 38.0 percent of those with the lowest scores (under 71) to 21.2 percent of those with the highest scores (above 85). The same pattern appears for multiple charges: 14.8 percent of subjects in the lowest Recruit Score range had two or more Trials, ranging down to 5.8 percent of those in the top range. The relationship between Recruit Score and Trials attained statistical significance in the regression analysis.

Recruit Score was even more strongly associated with Substantiated Com-

Table 4-23
Recruit Score vs. Career Type: Total Active Cohort

Recruit Score	Career Type																			
	Patrol		Temporarily Special		Traffic		Special		Detective Candidate		Detective Third Grade		Sergeant		Promoted Detective		Higher Promotion		Total	
	N	%	N	%	N	%	N	%	N	%	N	%	N	%	N	%	N	%	N	%
68-70	44	36.4	12	9.9	41	33.9	10	8.3	2	1.7	4	3.3	3	2.5	4	3.3	1	0.8	121	100.0
71-74	129	36.9	58	16.6	56	16.0	23	6.6	10	2.9	34	9.7	18	5.1	18	5.1	4	1.1	350	100.0
75-81	260	33.6	118	15.2	94	12.1	67	8.7	13	1.7	76	9.8	84	10.9	43	5.6	19	2.5	774	100.0
82-85	55	25.6	36	16.7	20	9.3	12	5.6	4	1.9	20	9.3	35	16.3	15	7.0	18	8.4	215	100.0
86-94	19	18.3	6	5.8	6	5.8	6	5.8	7	6.7	13	12.5	22	21.2	4	3.8	21	20.2	104	100.0
Total	507	32.4	230	14.7	217	13.9	118	7.5	36	2.3	147	9.4	162	10.4	84	5.4	63	4.0	1564	100.0

$\chi^2 = 218.7$ with 32 d.f., $p < .001$.

Table 4-24
Recruit Score vs. Trials: Total Active Cohort

Recruit Score	Trials										
	None		1		2		3		4+		Total
	N	%	N	%	N	%	N	%	N	%	N	%
68-70	75	62.0	28	23.1	12	9.9	1	.8	5	4.1	121	100.0
71-74	229	65.4	81	23.1	18	5.1	11	3.1	11	3.1	350	100.0
75-81	546	70.5	161	20.8	41	5.3	14	1.8	12	1.6	774	100.0
82-85	161	74.9	40	18.6	9	4.2	2	.9	3	1.4	215	100.0
86-94	82	78.8	16	15.4	6	5.8	–	–	–	–	104	100.0
Total	1093	69.9	326	20.8	86	5.5	28	1.8	31	2.0	1564	100.0

When grouped, $\chi^2 = 22.36$ with 9 d.f., $p < .01$

plaints than it was with Trials, since nearly all of the men with low recruit scores who were brought to departmental trial had at least one complaint against them substantiated, while the same was true for only 16 of the 22 men with high scores who were brought to trial. The relationship between Recruit Score and the final status of charges is shown in Table 4-25. When Recruit Score was entered into the regression equation for Substantiated Complaints, it was found to be the second most powerful predictor, after Unsatisfactory Probation.

For the most part, the higher incidence of misconduct among men with low recruit scores consisted of violations of the Department's rules and procedures; Recruit Score also attained statistical significance in the regression equation for Departmental Charges. However, the subjects with low recruit scores were not

Table 4-25
Recruit Score vs. Substantiated Complaints: Total Active Cohort

Recruit Score	Substantiated Complaints							
	No Complaints		Unsubstantiated Complaints		Substantiated Complaints		Total	
	N	%	N	%	N	%	N	%
68-70	43	35.5	32	26.4	46	38.0	121	100.0
71-74	148	42.3	85	24.3	117	33.5	350	100.0
75-81	320	41.3	250	32.3	204	26.4	774	100.0
82-85	92	42.8	72	33.5	51	23.7	215	100.0
86-94	54	51.9	34	32.7	16	15.4	104	100.0

$\chi^2 = 26.67$ with 8 d.f., $p < .001$

substantially higher than average on Civilian Complaints, and they were not at all higher on Criminal Complaints.

Recruit Score vs. Awards

The grades of subjects in the police academy were strongly related to the number of Awards they obtained subsequently. Those men who had the highest recruit scores are particularly notable in this regard, since 21.2 percent of them obtained five or more awards, compared to 12.0 percent on average. Only 8 out of 121 men with scores below 71 (6.6 percent) had more than five awards. The entire cross-tabulation is shown in Table 4-26.

Recruit Score vs. Times Sick

Subjects with high recruit scores had significantly less later absenteeism than subjects with low scores. This relationship is displayed in Table 4-27, which shows that the proportion of men with 11 or more Times Sick in 11 years ranged from 48.4 percent of those with Recruit Score under 71 down to 26.7 percent of those with scores over 85. Recruit Score emerged as the most powerful predictor in the regression equation for Times Sick, giving a correlation of .119.

Recruit Score vs. Performance: Black Subcohort

The recruit training scores of the black officers, unlike those of their white counterparts, were not significantly related to most performance measures, including Awards, Disciplinary Actions, and Absenteeism. They were related, however, to Career Type, and the patterns here were about the same as for whites.

We found that 45.1 percent of the officers with Recruit Scores of 75 and higher advanced to the Detective Division, compared to 9.7 percent of the officers with scores below 75, or four-and-a-half times as many. Not a single black officer with recruit training score of less than 75 advanced through civil service promotion. When entered into the regression equation, together with all other background factors, Recruit Score emerged as the most powerful predictor of Career Type for blacks and produced a correlation coefficient of .253, which was statistically significant at the .05 level. Recruit Score alone explained 6.4 percent of the variance of Career Type.

The overall incidence of misconduct for black officers, although not significantly related to Recruit Score, appeared to be consistent with the patterns

Table 4-26
Recruit Score vs. Awards: Total Active Cohort

Recruit Score	Awards													
	None		1		2		3		4		5+		Total	
	Number	Percent	Number	Percent	Number	Percent	Number	Percent	Number	Percent	Number	Percent	Number	Percent
68-70	40	33.1	40	33.1	18	14.9	11	9.1	4	3.3	8	6.6	121	100.0
71-74	97	27.7	96	27.4	60	17.1	37	10.6	20	5.7	40	11.4	350	100.0
75-81	250	32.3	190	24.6	116	15.0	76	9.8	51	6.6	90	11.6	773	100.0
82-85	59	27.4	44	20.5	29	13.5	39	18.1	17	7.9	27	12.6	215	100.0
86-94	25	24.0	29	27.9	17	16.3	4	3.8	7	6.7	22	21.2	104	100.0
Total	471	30.1	399	25.5	240	15.4	167	10.7	99	6.3	187	12.0	1563	100.0

$\chi^2 = 41.2$ with 20 d.f., $p < .005$

Table 4-27
Recruit Score vs. Times Sick: Total Active Cohort

Recruit Score	Times Sick									
	0-5		0-10		11-30		Over 30		Total	
	Number	Percent	Number	Percent	Number	Percent	Number	Percent	Number	Percent
68-70	27	22.5	35	29.2	50	41.7	8	6.7	120	100.0
71-74	103	9.6	92	26.4	143	41.1	10	2.9	348	100.0
75-81	260	33.9	227	29.6	258	33.6	23	3.0	768	100.0
82-85	80	37.4	56	26.2	70	32.7	8	3.7	214	100.0
86-94	43	42.6	31	30.7	27	26.7	0	—	101	100.0
Total	513	33.1	441	28.4	548	35.3	49	3.2	1551	100.0

$\chi^2 = 26.91$ with 12 d.f., $p < .01$

observed for the total cohort (i.e., the cross-tabulations for blacks could have arisen from a random sampling out of the total cohort).

Unsatisfactory Probation vs. Performance

Subjects with poor probationary ratings had a higher incidence of misconduct than average, but they did not differ from the norm in Awards or Career Type. The statistics show that subjects with poor probationary ratings had more allegations of misconduct, of which more were brought to trial and substantiated, than subjects without poor ratings. We found that 66.6 percent of the subjects with derogatory ratings had been alleged to have engaged in misconduct, compared to 54.8 percent of the subjects without negative ratings (see Table 4-28). Moreover, 37.7 percent and 35.2 percent, respectively, of the subjects with poor probationary ratings were brought to trial and received substantiated complaints. The corresponding proportions for officers without poor evaluations were 26.2 percent and 24.4 percent, respectively. When Unsatisfactory Probation was entered into each of the regression equations for Total Complaints, Trials, and Substantiated Complaints, it emerged as the most powerful predictor.

The higher incidence of misconduct for officers with poor probationary ratings resulted from more allegations of Department violations, but was not due to higher rates of civilian complaints, complaints characterizable as corruption, or harassment complaints. We found, for example, that 51.4 percent of those with an unsatisfactory mark on probation had at least one departmental allegation, compared to 41.1 percent of those with no unsatisfactory marks. When Unsatisfactory Probation was entered into the regression equation for Departmental Charges, it emerged as the most powerful predictor.

Subjects with poor probationary ratings tended to be absent more frequently than average. We found, for example, that 43.3 percent of the subjects with poor probationary ratings reported more than ten Times Sick, compared to only 35.8

Table 4-28
Unsatisfactory Probation vs. Total Complaints: Total Cohort

Unsatisfactory Probation	Total Complaints										
	None		1		2		3		4+		Total
0	493	45.2	288	26.4	156	14.3	80	7.3	74	6.8	1091	100.0
1	165	34.6	150	31.4	68	14.3	35	7.3	59	12.4	477	100.0
2+	2	9.1	7	31.8	2	9.1	4	18.2	7	31.8	22	100.0
Total	660	41.5	445	28.0	226	14.2	119	7.5	140	8.8	1590	100.0

$\chi^2 = 46.77$ with 8 d.f., $p < .001$

percent of the subjects without negative ratings. This relationship also attained statistical significance in the regression analysis.

In 1957, only 27 men (5 of whom later left the Department) were given 2 or more unsatisfactory marks on probation. Of these, 20 men also were graded below average on the recruit training score. If these 20 had been dropped from the Department, we may ask how many would have been falsely rejected, i.e., how many subsequently were good performers. One answer is that *none* of the men with unsatisfactory probation who subsequently had no charges of misconduct would have been rejected by this procedure. Also, none of the men who subsequently became detectives would have been rejected. (None of the men with 2 or more unsatisfactory marks on probation attained civil service promotions in any event.) It therefore appears that such a procedure will reject bad performers with very little risk of falsely rejecting good ones.

Unsatisfactory Probation vs. Performance: Black Subcohort

For the black officers, the relationship between probationary evaluation and police performance was almost identical to that for the total cohort. Unsatisfactory Probation was found to be a good predictor of above average incidence of later departmental misconduct and absenteeism, but it was not related to other performance variables. Unsatisfactory Probation was the strongest predictor in the regression equation for Departmental Charges among the blacks, producing a correlation coefficient of .225. The relationship between these two variables is displayed in more detail in Table 4-29.

The relationship between Unsatisfactory Probation and Times Sick for blacks, shown in Table 4-30, is also similar in all respects to that for whites, but is not statistically significant.

Table 4-29
Unsatisfactory Probation vs. Departmental Charges: Black Actives

Unsatisfactory Probation	Departmental Charges									
	None		1		2		3+		Total	
	N	%	N	%	N	%	N	%	N	%
0	22	40.7	16	29.6	11	20.4	5	9.3	54	100.0
1+	10	23.3	16	37.2	5	11.6	12	27.9	43	100.0
Total	32	33.0	32	33.0	16	16.5	17	17.5	97	100.0

$\chi^2 = 8.494$ with 3 d.f., $p < .05$

Table 4-30
Unsatisfactory Probationary vs. Times Sick: Black Actives

Unsatisfactory Probation	Times Sick							
	0-5		6-10		11+		Total	
0	24	45.3	14	26.4	15	28.3	53	100.0
1+	14	32.6	9	20.9	20	46.5	43	100.0
Total	38	39.6	23	24.0	35	36.6	96	100.0

χ^2 = 3.428 with 2 d.f., not significant.

Marksmanship vs. Performance

Marksmanship was found to be a statistically significant, but not very strong, predictor of Career Type and later Disciplinary Actions. Expert marksmanship was also associated with a higher number of Awards, but this may be attributed to the fact that a citation is given to a police officer who qualifies as an expert. For blacks, the patterns were similar but not statistically significant.

Marksmanship vs. Career Type

The cross-tabulation of Marksmanship with Career Type showed that expert marksmen were more likely to attain civil service promotions than other officers, but they were not more likely to become detectives. Sixteen percent of the expert marksmen were sergeants, lieutenants, or captains after fourteen years on the force, compared to 9.2 percent of the non-experts. In the New York City Police Department, officers may be granted extra points on their promotion examination scores for marksmanship, but we believe that the number of points awarded in this way is too small to explain the observed variations in Marksmanship vs. Career Type. Marksmanship attained significance at the .05 level in the regression equation for Career Type, but its contribution to reduction of variance was very small.

Marksmanship vs. Disciplinary Actions

Expert marksmen had slightly lower counts of Total Complaints, Trials, and Substantiated Complaints than average. We found, for example, that 28.2 percent of the expert marksmen were brought to trial for allegations of misconduct, compared to 34.0 percent of the non-experts. This small difference is typical of all three of the relationships between Marksmanship and the indicators of misconduct.

Precinct Hazard vs. Performance

The hazard status of the precinct where officers are first assigned was of interest to us as a predictor variable, since it might reveal the extent to which later performance is related to early experience as a policeman. As can be seen from the absence of any correlations with Precinct Hazard in Table 3-16, white officers were apparently not assigned to precincts in accordance with any of their background characteristics, and therefore Precinct Hazard is essentially an independent predictor variable. Typically, each officer spent at least two years in the precinct where he was first assigned (many are still in the same precinct), which seemed to be an adequate length of time for influences on later performance to appear, if there were any.

The results of the analysis were that even the statistically significant differences in Precinct Hazard vs. Performance were not so large as to be very interesting. For example, the men initially assigned to the highest hazard precincts accumulated significantly more Total Complaints than their counterparts in average hazard precincts, but the differences were as follows: 59.8 percent of subjects initially in high and extreme hazard precincts had one or more complaints, compared to 51.2 percent of those initially in average hazard precincts. Similarly, Precinct Hazard was found to be a significant predictor in the regression equation for Civilian Complaints, but Table 4-31 shows that whatever differences exist are very small, especially in regard to complaints of the use of unnecessary force.

We did find, however, that the hazard status of the precinct of first assignment had no effect on the career advancement of officers and was not associated with later Awards, Sick Time, or allegations of corruption or harassment.

Current Residence vs. Performance

Although all the subjects were required to live in New York City when they joined the force in 1957, by 1968 some 45.9 percent had moved elsewhere. In light of the recent controversy in several states over whether police officers should reside in their city of employment, it is interesting to see how those who moved outside the City differ in performance from those who remained.

Since the data in this study cover an eleven-year period, and we did not determine the date at which each officer moved, the performance measures are partly derived from years when the men lived in the City and partly from later

Table 4-31
Precinct Hazard vs. Civilian Complaints: Total Active Cohort

Precinct Hazard	Civilian Complaints											
	No Civilian Complaints		One Complaint of Abuse of Authority Discourtesy or Ethnic Slurs		1 Complaint of The Use of Un-necessary Force		2 Complaints of Abuse of Authority Discourtesy or Ethnic Slurs		2 Complaints; One Unnecessary Force		Total	
	N	%	N	%	N	%	N	%	N	%	N	%
Average	207	80.2	14	5.4	25	9.7	2	.8	10	3.9	258	100.0
High	223	78.0	24	8.4	22	7.7	3	1.0	14	4.9	286	100.0
Extreme	665	74.4	84	9.4	88	9.8	13	1.5	44	4.9	894	100.0
Total	1095	76.1	122	8.5	135	9.7	18	1.3	68	4.7	1438	100.0

$\chi^2 = 7.214$ with 8 d.f., $p \simeq .5$ (not significant)

years. Nonetheless, it is possible to draw certain conclusions about the men who moved.

First, one might hypothesize that the fraction of men moving out of the City would vary with annual salary, but this was not the case. Although 52.9 percent of lieutenants and captains had moved outside the City (compared to 44 percent on average), only 36.5 percent of the promoted detectives had moved, and their salaries are roughly comparable. These two groups taken together were about average in terms of their fraction of non-City residents. The fraction of third grade detectives and sergeants who had moved out of the City was almost exactly the same as the fraction of patrolmen who moved (45.2 percent vs. 43.6 percent). Among black officers, however, we did observe a pattern of greater movement out of the City at higher salaries. In fact, half of all the black officers who resided outside the City were detectives or sergeants.

The only interesting difference between the City residents and those who moved outside was that the non-City residents reported sick more frequently. This is probably related to the fact that reports of illness to the Police Department surgeon by non-City residents cannot be as rapidly verified. We found that 42.2 percent of officers living outside the City reported ill eleven or more times in eleven years, compared to 35.1 percent of the City residents. See Table 4-32. This pattern was not observed for the black officers.

Among the black officers, a higher number of awards were won by non-City residents than City residents. See Table 4-33. This is entirely explained by the fact, noted above, that black detectives tended to move out of the City; in general detectives win more awards than other officers.

Differences between City residents and non-City residents in terms of Disciplinary Actions were quite small and, on balance, did not suggest that either group performed better in this regard. In sum, the data available to us are

Table 4-32
Current Residence vs. Times Sick: Total Active Cohort

| Current Residence | Times Sick | | | | | | | | | |
| | 0-5 | | 6-10 | | 11-30 | | 31+ | | Total | |
	N	%	N	%	N	%	N	%	N	%
Outside New York City	213	30.5	191	27.3	266	38.1	29	4.1	699	100.0
Inside New York City	316	35.7	259	29.2	290	32.7	21	2.4	886	100.0
Total	529	33.4	450	28.4	556	35.1	50	3.2	1585	100.0

$\chi^2 = 10.733$ with 3 d.f., $p < .01$

Table 4-33
Current Residence vs. Awards: Black Actives

Current Residence	None		1		2		3		4		5		Total	
	Number	Percent	Number	Percent	Number	Percent	Number	Percent	Number	Percent	Number	Percent	Number	Percent
Outside NYC	4	18.2	7	31.8	3	13.6	0	–	3	13.6	5	22.7	22	100.0
Inside NYC	23	30.3	26	34.2	9	11.8	10	13.2	3	3.9	5	6.6	76	100.0
Total	27	27.6	33	33.7	12	12.2	10	10.2	6	6.1	10	10.2	98	100.0

Awards

somewhat unsatisfactory for analysis of the effect of residence, but they do not suggest that police officers who live outside New York City differ from resident policemen in any aspect of performance other than absenteeism.

5

Predicting Police Performance

In this chapter we are interested in three objectives. First, we wish to identify the relative importance of each background factor (independent variable) by relating each to individual performance measures, always holding constant the remaining factors. Second, we wish to predict the value of certain variables (the performance measures) from a separate set of variables (background factors). In the process, we can determine how much of the total variation in the performance variable can be explained by a combination of the independent variables working together. Third, we will develop a single general performance index derived from the individual performance measures and discuss how well it can be predicted.

The statistical technique we used for these tasks was stepwise multiple linear regression, in which the most powerful background factor enters the regression equation first and explains as much of the variance of the performance measure as it can. This is followed by the second strongest independent factor, and so forth. Whenever a new factor is introduced, each of the preceding factors is held constant to avoid duplication. The assumptions underlying the use of linear regression are described in any standard textbook on the subject.[44]

The computer program utilized for this analysis (SPSS) permits identification, by F test, of the statistical significance of the reduction in variance produced by each independent variable. We retained only those predictor variables whose contribution was significantly different from zero at the .05 level. Thus, the regression equation for the performance variable Y takes the form

- ineffective officer - what are factors that predicted

$$Y = a + b_1 X_1 + b_2 X_2 + \ldots + b_k X_k,$$

where the number k of predictor variables included (and the particular variables included) varies with the performance measure.

The following background variables were used as independent factors in each regression equation: Age, I.Q., Education, Region of Birth, Father's Occupation, Last Occupation, Siblings, Marital Status, Children, Residences, Jobs, Debts, Military Record, Military Commendations, Arrest History, Court Appearances, Summonses, Employment Discipline, Military Discipline, Civil Service, Background Rating, Recruit Score, Unsatisfactory Probation, Marksmanship, and Precinct Hazard. See Chapter 3 for detailed descriptions of these variables.

The dependent variables we attempt to predict are the following performance measures:

101

1. Career Type
2. Awards
3. Total Complaints
4. Trials
5. Substantiated Complaints
6. Departmental Charges
7. Civilian Complaints
8. Criminal Complaints
9. Harassment
10. Sick Time
11. Injury Disapproval
12. Firearms Removal
13. General Performance Index.

Findings

The results of the regression analysis between background factors and individual performance measures for white and black officers are summarized in Tables 5-1 and 5-2. All the performance measures whose multiple correlation with background variables was significantly different from zero at the .05 level are shown on these tables, in order of their multiple correlation. None of the other performance variables had a significant multiple correlation. There were 41 statistically significant relationships, 35 for the total active cohort (which we interpret as typical of the white officers) and 6 for the black subjects. The multiple correlation coefficients (R) shown on the tables are not large, but, as we pointed out in Chapter 2, larger multiple correlations are rarely found in studies of this type, while it is common to find correlations that fail to pass significance tests.

Table 5-1 shows, for example, that there were six statistically significant relationships between background factors and Career Type for the white officers. This performance variable had the highest multiple correlation found in this study ($R = .328$). Recruit Score, the most powerful factor, entered the regression equation first, yielding a correlation coefficient of .241, which explained 5.8 percent of the variance in Career Type. The table indicates that the sign of beta for the variable Recruit Score was positive, which means that higher scores in the training academy were associated with better career types. Civil Service entered the regression equation next as the second strongest predictor and accounted for an additional 2.6 percent of the variance. The third strongest predictor after Recruit Score and Civil Service was Age, which yielded a multiple correlation coefficient of .308 and explained an additional 1.1 percent of the variation. Three more relationships involving Marksmanship, Region of Birth, and Last Occupation were statistically significant and increased

Table 5-1
Regression Results: Total Active Cohort

Performance Measure	Background Variable	R	R^2	Change in R^2	Sign of Beta	Signif.
	Recruit Score	.241	5.8%	5.8%	+	.001
	Civil Service	.290	8.4%	2.6%	+	.001
	Age	.308	9.5%	1.1%	−	.001
Career Type	Marksmanship	.316	10.0%	0.5%	+	.05
	Region of Birth	.322	10.4%	0.4%	+	.05
	Last Occupation	.328	10.8%	0.4%	+	.05
	Unsatisfactory Probation	.192	3.7%	3.7%	+	.001
	Recruit Score	.216	4.7%	1.0%	−	.001
Substantiated	Military Discipline	.234	5.5%	0.8%	+	.01
Complaints	Employment Disciplinary Record	.243	5.9%	0.4%	+	.05
	Marksmanship	.250	6.3%	0.4%	−	.05
	Unsatisfactory Probation	.187	3.5%	3.5%	+	.001
	Military Discipline	.201	4.0%	0.5%	+	.01
Trials	Marksmanship	.213	4.5%	0.5%	−	.05
	Recruit Score	.222	4.9%	0.4%	−	.05
	Unsatisfactory Probation	.167	2.8%	2.8%	+	.001
Departmental	Background Rating	.195	3.8%	1.0%	−	.001
Charges	Recruit Score	.207	4.3%	0.5%	−	.05
	Employment Disciplinary Record	.216	4.7%	0.4%	+	.05
	Recruit Score	.119	1.4%	1.4%	−	.001
Times Sick	Age	.141	2.0%	0.6%	−	.01
	Background Rating	.156	2.4%	0.4%	−	.05
	Unsatisfactory Probation	.166	2.8%	0.4%	+	.05
Total	Unsatisfactory Probation	.142	2.0%	2.0%	+	.001
Complaints	Military Discipline	.156	2.4%	0.4%	+	.001
	Marksmanship	.165	2.7%	0.3%	−	.05
	Recruit Score	.078	0.6%	0.6%	+	.01
Awards	Summonses	.103	1.1%	0.5%	+	.05
	I.Q.	.118	1.4%	0.3%	+	.05
	Military Record	.131	1.7%	0.3%	+	.05
Civilian	Education	.078	0.6%	0.6%	−	.01
Complaints	Age	.100	1.0%	0.4%	−	.05
	Precinct Hazard	.116	1.3%	0.3%	+	.05
Harassment	Court Appearances	.089	0.8%	0.8%	+	.01
	Arrest History	.107	1.1%	0.3%	−	.01

Table 5-2
Regression Results: Black Actives

Performance Measure	Background Variable	R	R^2	Change in R^2	Sign of Beta	Signif.
Trials	Siblings	.254	6.4%	6.4%	−	.05
	I.Q.	.346	12.0%	5.6%	+	.05
Career Type	Recruit Score	.253	6.4%	6.4%	+	.05
	Region of Birth	.341	11.6%	5.2%	+	.05
Civilian Complaints	Court Appearances	.263	6.9%	6.9%	+	.05
Departmental Charges	Unsatisfactory Probation	.255	6.5%	6.5%	+	.05

the multiple correlation coefficient to .328. However, the portion of unexplained variation that was rendered explained never exceeded 0.5 percent for any of these three factors.

The next two strongest predictors of Career Type after Last Occupation were I.Q. and Education (not shown in Table 5-1). Together they explained less than 0.5 percent of the variance in Career Type and failed to attain statistical significance. However, the data from the regression analysis show that had either factor been forced into the regression equation before the stronger predictor Civil Service, it would have explained a sufficient portion of the variance to have attained statistical significance. Since these factors were correlated with Civil Service, their contribution was suppressed by Civil Service. Thus, although the addition of I.Q. or education was not statistically significant in the present study, either factor would be a suitable surrogate for Civil Service to predict Career Type. (Factors which were similarly suppressed in the other regression equations are discussed in Appendix C.)

Continuing to the next item in Table 5-1, we observe that the second highest multiple correlation coefficient produced for the total active cohort was in the regression equation involving Substantiated Complaints ($R = .250$). Five relationships between background factors and Substantiated Complaints were statistically significant. They include, in order of power of prediction, Unsatisfactory Probation, Recruit Score, Military Discipline, Employment Discipline, and Marksmanship. The most powerful predictor, Unsatisfactory Probation, produced a correlation coefficient of .192 and explained 3.7 percent of the variance in Substantiated Complaints. All the factors significantly related to Substantiated Complaints could be identified by the background investigators or by evaluation of performance during the first nine months of an officer's appointment.

The next two performance variables, in order of their multiple correlation for the total cohort, were Trials and Departmental Charges. These two are closely related to each other and to Substantiated Complaints, since the bulk of complaints brought to trial are departmental complaints, and over 80 percent of such complaints brought to trial are substantiated. In each case, the predictors that were significant contributors to reducing the variance of Trials or Departmental Charges were also significant for Substantiated Complaints, except that Background Rating was somewhat stronger than Military Discipline as a predictor for Departmental Charges.

Further down the list is Civilian Complaints, which is seen to have an entirely different collection of significant predictors. (This explains in part the fact that Total Complaints, which is the sum of Civilian Complaints, Criminal Complaints, and Departmental Charges, has a lower multiple correlation coefficient than some of its components.) The background characteristics significantly related to Civilian Complaints are not those ordinarily counted as negative by background investigators or superior officers evaluating a recruit's performance on probation. Instead, the older, better educated men had fewer civilian complaints, and those officers initially placed in precincts where civilian complaints are most frequent naturally accumulated more of them.

A man's future absenteeism proved to be somewhat predictable during his probationary period, but his future record of awards seemed to be less identifiable from any meaningful combination of characteristics.

The highest multiple correlation attained for the black subjects (Table 5-2) was .346, which explained a total of 12 percent in the variation of the number of Trials. The only two factors to attain statistical significance, in order of their strength of prediction, were Siblings and I.Q. The number of siblings was inversely associated with complaints brought to trial and alone produced a correlation coefficient of .254, which explained 6.4 percent of the variation. When I.Q. entered the regression equation, it accounted for an additional 5.6 percent of the variance. In two of the regression equations for the black subjects, only one background factor made a significant reduction in the variance. The two equations involved the dependent variables Civilian Complaints and Departmental Charges. We found that the correlation between Court Appearances and Civilian Complaints yielded a correlation coefficient of .263, which explained 6.9 percent of the variance. Similarly, the only relationship of statistical significance for Departmental Charges was its association with Unsatisfactory Probation. The correlation coefficient was .255, and Unsatisfactory Probation explained 6.5 percent of the variation in Departmental Charges.

Background Factors as Predictors

The background factors found to be statistically significant in one or more of the regression equations were ordered for both white and black officers by the maximum amount of variation it explained. (See Table 5-3.) We found for the white subjects that Recruit Score was the most powerful predictor, by virtue of its contribution to reduction of variance in Career Type and its appearance as a significant factor in five other regressions. Similarly, Court Appearances emerged as the strongest predictor for the black subjects, because it reduced the variance in Civilian Complaints by 6.9 percent. None of the background factors attained statistical significance with more than one performance measure in regressions using data for the black subjects only. The second strongest predictor, regardless of race, was Unsatisfactory Probation, which explained 3.7 percent and 6.5 percent of the variance, respectively, in Substantiated Complaints for the white subjects and Departmental Charges for the black subjects.

Five of the six background factors that attained statistical significance in a regression for the black subjects also were significant for the whites. These factors included Unsatisfactory Probation, Recruit Score, I.Q., Region of Birth, and Court Appearances. However, for I.Q., an increasing score was related to effective performance for the white subjects but ineffective performance for the blacks. We found that white officers with high I.Q.s won more awards than average, while black officers with high I.Q.s tended to be brought to trial for misconduct more frequently than their lower scoring counterparts. The single factor that attained statistical significance for the black subjects but not the whites was Siblings, which emerged as the best predictor of Trials. Three of the background variables made a comparatively substantial contribution in one or more of the regressions for the whites but were not significant for the blacks. These were Civil Service, Age, and Background.

The variables that did not emerge as significant in any of the regression equations were Father's Occupation, Jobs, Marital Status, Children, Debts, Residences, and Military Commendations.

Predicting Performance Measures

To indicate the extent to which performance measures would be expected to vary, depending on background characteristics of candidates, we have calculated some typical values of performance measures from the regression equations. In the case of the variable Career Type, the regression equation for the total cohort was

$$
\begin{aligned}
\text{Career Type} \;=\; & 1.19 \\
&+ \; 0.093 \times (\text{Recruit Score} - 68) \\
&+ \; 0.084 \times (\text{Civil Service} - 70) \\
&- \; 0.083 \times (\text{Age} - 21) \\
&+ \; 0.387 \times (\text{Marksmanship}).
\end{aligned}
$$

Table 5-3
Background Factors as Predictors

	Total Active Cohort			Active Blacks	
Variable	Maximum R^2	Number of Associations	Variable	Maximum R^2	Number of Associations
Recruit Score	5.8%	6	Court Appearances	6.9%	1
Unsatisfactory Probation	3.7%	5	Unsatisfactory Probation	6.5%	1
Civil Service	2.6%	1	Siblings	6.4%	1
Age	1.1%	3	Recruit Score	6.4%	1
Background Rating	1.0%	2	I.Q.	5.5%	1
Court Appearances	0.8%	1	Region of Birth	5.2%	1
Military Discipline	0.8%	3			
Education	0.6%	1			
Marksmanship	0.5%	3			
Summonses	0.5%	1			
Employment Disciplinary Record	0.4%	2			
Region of Birth	0.4%	1			
Arrest History	0.3%	1			
I.Q.	0.3%	1			
Military Service	0.3%	1			
Precinct Hazard	0.3%	1			
Last Occupation	0.3%	1			

Although no real meaning can be attached to values of Career Type which are not integers, it is reasonable to say that about half of the candidates with a given combination of characteristics would be expected to rank at least as high as the assignment whose code corresponds to the calculated value of Career Type, rounded to an integer. For purpose of interpretation, we remind the reader of the order in which we classified assignments:

Code	Assignment
0	Patrol
1	Temporarily Special
2	Traffic
3	Special
4	Detective Candidate
5	Detective Third Grade
6	Sergeant Only
7	Promoted Detective
8	Higher Promotion

Table 5-4 shows the ranks we would expect to be attained or surpassed fourteen years later by half of the candidates with specified Age, Civil Service,

Table 5-4
Expected Rank 14 Years Later for Candidates with Specified Scores

	Age = 21		
	Recruit Score		
Civil Service	68	80	90
70	Temporarily Special	Traffic	Special
80	Traffic	Special	Detective Candidate
90	Special	Detective Candidate	Detective Third Grade
	Age = 31		
	Recruit Score		
Civil Service	68	80	90
70	Patrol	Temp. Special or Traffic	Traffic or Special
80	Temporarily Special	Traffic	Special
90	Traffic	Special	Detective Candidate

and Recruit Score. For example, over half of the men aged 21 at appointment whose civil service score was 90 or higher and whose recruit training score was 90 or higher would be expected to attain the ranks of detective, sergeant, lieutenant, or captain. By contrast, more than half of the men aged 31 with the lowest passing grades on the civil service exam and the recruit academy exams would be in precinct patrol fourteen years later.

After Career Type, the next most predictable performance measure was Substantiated Complaints. The regression equation was

$$
\begin{aligned}
\text{Substantiated Complaints} = \ & 0.457 \\
& + 0.280 \times (\text{Unsatisfactory Probation}) \\
& - 0.014 \times (\text{Recruit Score} - 68) \\
& + 0.082 \times (\text{Military Discipline}) \\
& + 0.099 \times (\text{Employment Discipline}) \\
& - 0.101 \times (\text{Marksmanship}).
\end{aligned}
$$

The results implied by this equation are shown in Table 5-5. (As an approximation, we replaced the coefficients of both Military Discipline and Employment Discipline by 0.09.) We see from this table that candidates with three military or employment disciplinary incidents, the lowest possible recruit score, and two "unsatisfactory" marks on their probation reports would be expected to have 8.5 times as many Substantiated Complaints as men with no military or employment discipline, a Recruit Score of 90, and no "unsatisfactory" marks on probation.

Table 5-5

Expected Average Number of Substantiated Complaints 11 Years Later for Candidates with Specified Scores

Unsatisfactory Probation	No military or employment discipline		
	Recruit Score		
	68	80	90
None	0.46	0.29	0.15
2 "Unsatisfactory" Marks	1.00	0.83	0.69
Unsatisfactory Probation	3 military + employment discipline		
	Recruit Score		
	68	80	90
None	0.73	0.56	0.42
2 "Unsatisfactory" Marks	1.27	1.10	0.96

A similar disparity is found for Civilian Complaints between older college graduates and younger high school graduates. (See Table 5-6.) The regression equation was

$$\text{Civilian Complaints} = 0.336$$
$$- \ 0.069 \times (\text{Education})$$
$$- \ 0.014 \times (\text{Age} - 21)$$
$$+ \ 0.050 \times (\text{Precinct Hazard}).$$

acct for civilian interaction

We will not display the results from the regression equations for the other Disciplinary Actions variables, since they are similar to, but weaker than, the one for Substantiated Complaints. However, the variable Times Sick also shows some interesting patterns, which are displayed in Table 5-7. Here the regression equation is

$$\text{Times Sick} = 13.413$$
$$- \ \ 0.170 \times (\text{Recruit Score} - 68)$$
$$- \ \ 0.214 \times (\text{Age} - 21)$$
$$- \ \ 0.686 \times (\text{Background Rating})$$
$$+ \ \ 0.939 \times (\text{Unsatisfactory Probation}).$$

We see from the table that young men with low recruit scores and poor background and probation ratings will have nearly three times as much absenteeism as older men with high recruit scores and high ratings.

Multiple Correlation Coefficients

The final multiple correlation coefficients that emerged *after all the background factors were entered* into the regression equation with each performance measure for the total active cohort and black actives are presented in Table 5-8. We found that despite the relatively high coefficients for the black subjects (e.g., 0.623 for Trials; 0.606 for Substantiated Complaints), not a single one was

Table 5-6
Expected Number of Civilian Complaints 11 Years Later for Candidates with Specified Age and Education*

	Age		
Education	21	27	31
High School Graduate	0.47	0.39	0.34
College Graduate	0.20	0.12	0.07

— 7 out of 100

*All men are assumed to be assigned to "extreme" hazard precincts.

Table 5-7
Expected Times Sick in 11 Years for Candidates with Specified Characteristics

	Background Rating = Disapproval or Poor 2 Unsatisfactory Marks on Probation		
	Recruit Score		
Age	68	80	90
21	15.29	13.25	11.55
27	14.01	12.07	10.27
31	13.15	11.11	9.41

	Background Rating = Excellent No Unsatisfactory Marks on Probation		
	Recruit Score		
Age	68	80	90
21	11.36	9.32	7.62
27	10.07	8.03	6.33
31	9.21	7.17	5.47

Table 5-8
Multiple Correlation Coefficients for Total Active Cohort and Black Actives, All Background Factors Entered

	Total Active Cohort				Black Actives			
Variable	Rank	R	R^2	Signif.	Rank	R	R^2	Signif.
Career Type	1	.347	.121	.001	7	.505	.225	N.S.*
Substantiated Complaints	2	.279	.078	.001	2	.606	.367	N.S.
Trials	3	.258	.067	.001	1	.623	.389	N.S.
Departmental Charges	4	.257	.066	.001	3	.578	.344	N.S.
Total Complaints	5	.226	.051	.001	6	.519	.269	N.S.
Times Sick	6	.215	.046	.001	12	.420	.176	N.S.
Harassment	7	.175	.031	.05	10	.447	.200	N.S.
Awards	8	.172	.030	.05	8	.480	.230	N.S.
Civilian Complaints	9	.163	.027	N.S.*	5	.526	.277	N.S.
Injury Disapproval	10	.140	.019	N.S.	11	.422	.178	N.S.
Firearms Removed	11	.117	.014	N.S.	9	.453	.176	N.S.
Criminal Complaints	12	.113	.013	N.S.	4	.537	.289	N.S.

*N.S. = Not Significant

statistically significant. On the other hand, the majority of multiple correlation coefficients for the total actives attained statistical significance, although they were substantially lower in magnitude than the corresponding coefficients for their black counterparts. These results were due to differences in numbers of white and black subjects in the 1957 cohort. The data in Table 5-8 show, for example, that the final coefficient for Career Type, after all background factors were entered into the regression equation for all actives, was .347. This coefficient reduced the total unexplained variation by 12 percent and attained statistical significance at the .001 level. Similarly, the overall multiple correlation coefficient for Times Sick, for example, was .215 which accounted for 3 percent of the variation and was significant at the .001 level.

General Performance Index

With the thought that some subjects might score high on both positive and negative performance variables (e.g., a man could have a large number of Awards, rapid career advancement, and a large number of Departmental Charges), we felt it would be desirable to produce a performance index in which these effects would cancel out. In this way, we would be able to determine which background characteristics were associated with "unblemished" good performance, and which with "unredeemed" bad performance.

After trying several different combinations of the performance variables as general indices, we found that the relationship between background characteristics and the index was not very sensitive to its exact form. We therefore describe the results for a typical index, defined as follows:

$$
\begin{aligned}
\text{General Performance Index} \ = \ & 0.5 \times (\text{Awards}) \\
& - \ 0.05 \times (\text{Times Sick}) \\
& - \ 1 \times (\text{Injury Disapproval}) \\
& - \ 2 \times (\text{Firearms Removal}) \\
& - \ 1 \times (\text{Departmental Charges}) \\
& - \ 2 \times (\text{Civilian Complaints}) \\
& - \ 2 \times (\text{Criminal Complaints}) \\
& - \ 1 \times (\text{Substantiated Complaints}) \\
& + \ (\text{Extra points for promotions}).
\end{aligned}
$$

The points awarded for promotion were:

Detective Third Grade	1 point
Sergeant or Promoted Detective	2 points
Higher Promotion	3 points.

Note that any substantiated complaint is counted twice in the index; for example, a substantiated criminal complaint would subtract 3 from the performance index. The average score on the general performance index was −1.08 for the total cohort and −2.41 for blacks. The difference simply reflects the fact that blacks did not progress as far in the ranks as whites, and they received more charges of departmental misconduct.

The regression analysis for the total cohort showed that the same predictors that appeared strongly in the equations for individual performance measures also appeared in the equation for the general performance index, and therefore the possibility of a cancellation effect was not confirmed. For the blacks, such an effect may be present. The data from the regression analysis of the general performance index is presented in Table 5-9. We found that five predictors attained statistical significance in the regression equation for the white subjects. Recruit Score emerged as the strongest predictor, yielding a correlation coefficient of .181, and accounted for 3.3 percent of the variance. The next two strongest predictors were Unsatisfactory Probation and Civil Service, which together explained an additional 2.3 percent of the variation. Marksmanship entered the regression equation next, and finally Military Discipline, both of which accounted for less than 1 percent of the variation. In addition, I.Q. would have attained statistical significance had it entered the regression equation instead of Civil Service. (See Appendix C.)

The results of the regression equation for the overall performance index for the blacks were also similar to the results for the individual performance measures. When all background factors entered into the regression equation, Unsatisfactory Probation emerged as the strongest predictor, producing a correlation coefficient of .211, explaining 4.4 percent of the variation. However, unlike the regression equation for the individual measures, this relationship failed to attain statistical significance.

Table 5-9
Regression Results: General Performance Index

	Whites				Blacks				
Factor	R	R^2	Sign of Beta	Signif.	Factor	R	R^2	Sign of Beta	Signif.
Recruit Score	.181	3.3%	+	.001					
Unsat. Prob.	.213	1.3%	−	.001	Unsat. Prob.	.211	4.4%	−	N.S.*
Civil Service	.235	1.0%	+	.001					
Marksmanship	.246	0.5%	+	.01					
Military Disc.	.253	0.4%	−	.05					

*N.S. = Not Significant

These findings indicate that the measures used in this study do not permit development of a single equation for weighting the background variables and early performance scores of recruits to obtain a single predictor of overall later performance which is valid for both black and white officers. However, the general principles which should apply in deciding which recruits to terminate appear to be consistent for both races. Those recruits whose scores on examinations in the Police Academy are below passing should be dropped rather than given additional opportunities to pass. In addition, those whose probationary evaluation is unsatisfactory on several dimensions of performance should be terminated if their recruit score was also low. In questionable cases, the background characteristics of the recruit could be reviewed at the end of the probationary period to see whether he has a history of incidents found to be related to subsequent disciplinary actions. These include military or employment disciplinary incidents and multiple appearances in civil court.

Profiles of Subgroups of Police Officers

When a single background variable is found to be associated with two or more different performance measures, the explanation may be either that the several performance characteristics tend to be found together in any given officer or that the one background variable predicts distinct dimensions of performance. To distinguish between these possibilities, we have analyzed the correlations among the performance measures and developed profiles of the officers who have distinguishable performance patterns.

The simple Pearson correlation coefficients between pairs of performance measures are shown in Table 6-1 for the total active cohort. Only those correlations which exceeded .20 in magnitude are shown, and those variables which had no such correlations are omitted. The patterns for the black subcohort were nearly identical, and therefore are not shown separately. Some of the correlations are direct consequences of the definitions of the variables. For example, allegations of harassment are included in Departmental Charges, and these in turn are included in Total Complaints; therefore, Harassment correlates with these two variables. However, harassment charges were not brought to departmental trial, and were therefore not substantiated, so that Harassment does not correlate with Trials or Substantiated Complaints. Other types of departmental charges are, however, routinely brought to trial, and

Table 6-1
Performance Measures: Correlations × 100   **Total Active Cohort**

	Career Type	Awards	Harassment	Departmental Charges	Civilian Complaints	Total Complaints	Trials	Substantiated Complaints	Times Sick
Career Type	●								
Awards	28	●							
Harassment			●						
Departmental Charges			41	●					
Civilian Complaints					●				
Total Complaints			37	82	56	●			
Trials				78		72	●		
Substantiated Complaints	−20			78		64	86	●	
Times Sick	−22			28		29	32	29	●

115

therefore Departmental Charges correlates with Total Complaints, Trials, and Substantiated Complaints. Similar explanations apply for the other correlations among the Disciplinary Actions variables.

However, the remaining correlations have more substantive meaning. The correlation between Awards and Career Type reflects the fact that an officer must produce a large number of arrests to become a detective, and once he is a detective he spends most of his time on activities likely to result in arrests. Therefore, the detectives (who score 5 or 7 on Career Type) will have an above average number of Awards. We also see from Table 6-1 that men who have Substantiated Charges on their record tend to be retarded from further career advancement.

The correlations between Times Sick and the other variables are interesting because they tend to confirm that excessive absenteeism is in fact a bona fide characteristic of men with unsatisfactory performance, rather than simply indicating poorer health. Men with a large number of Times Sick also have above-average numbers of Departmental Charges (presumably for forms of misconduct other than absenteeism), and they have less satisfactory career advancement than other officers. However, a portion of the correlation between Times Sick and Career Type arises from the fact that detectives, who do not always work regular hours and are not subject to daily supervision, do not report sick officially as often as other officers.

For a better understanding of these intercorrelations, we performed a factor analysis on the matrix of correlations of all background and performance measures taken together. The program used was the SPSS factor analysis with Quartimax rotation.[45] The output of this program is a collection of factors, which are linear combinations of the variables, on which individual subjects tend to score either high or low. Variables that are essentially unrelated to the others will tend to appear in factors by themselves, while associated variables will appear together in single factors.

The results of this analysis for the total active cohort are displayed in Table 6-2. The factors are shown in order of the amount of the variance in the data which is accounted for by the factor. Those factors which explain more than 4 percent of the variance are listed. For each factor, the variables whose loadings were .20 or larger in magnitude are shown in the table, and the names of the factors were derived from inspecting these variables.

We see that the strongest factor is descriptive of an officer who is a discipline problem for the department, having a large number of Departmental Charges and Times Sick. As would be expected from the correlation matrix, the variables Harassment and Civilian Complaints, which also contribute to Total Complaints, are not present in this factor and therefore represent different dimensions of misconduct. Each of them appeared in its own separate factor.

The second factor is artificial, since it merely describes the fact that a man must be in the military in order to have a military disciplinary record.

Table 6-2
Factor Analysis: Total Active Cohort

Factor Name	Percent of Variance	Variables Which Load on Factor	Factor Matrix Coefficient
1. Departmental Discipline Problem	21.8	Trials	0.945
		Substantiated Complaints	0.888
		Departmental Charges	0.888
		Total Complaints	0.793
		Times Sick	0.318
2. Military Discipline	17.0	Military Record	
		Military Discipline	
3. Older, Married Stable	11.9	Marital Status	0.832
		Children	0.700
		Residences	0.603
		Age	0.558
		Debts	0.453
4. Intelligence	8.0	Civil Service	0.637
		I.Q.	0.584
		Recruit Score	0.452
		Career Type	0.256
5. Civilian Complaints	6.5	Civilian Complaints	0.799
		Total Complaints	0.542
6. Prior Criminal History	5.0	Arrest History	0.607
		Violent Offenses	0.542
7. Harassment	4.0	Harassment	0.756
		Departmental Charges	0.394
		Total Complaints	0.281

The third factor is descriptive of the older, married, stable applicant and shows that an above average number of debts is associated with these characteristics. This factor is unrelated to any of the performance factors. Thus, to the extent that excessive debts were found to be related to later unsatisfactory performance, it is only the presence of debts in the absence of these other characteristics that is worth taking into account.

The fourth factor, intelligence, is the only major factor that combined both background and performance variables. The variables that loaded heavily on this factor were Civil Service, I.Q., Recruit Score, and Career Type.

For the black actives, the patterns revealed by factor analysis were remarkably the same, but the differences are worth noting. (See Table 6-3.) First, the variable Siblings appears in a factor for the blacks (Departmental Discipline), whereas it is totally missing from the corresponding factor for the whites. (The loading of Siblings on Factor 1 for the total cohort was 0.003.) Second, the variables that constitute the factor descriptive of the intelligent white officer (Factor 4 for the total cohort) do not join in a coherent pattern for the blacks.

Police Performance Profiles

Using the results from our cross-tabulations and regression analysis, we can develop profiles of the candidates who are most likely to develop the per-

Table 6-3
Factor Analysis: Black Actives

Factor Name	Percent of Variance	Variables Which Load on Factor	Factor Matrix Coefficient
1. Departmental Discipline Problem	15.7	Substantiated Complaints	0.911
		Departmental Charges	0.902
		Total Complaints	0.727
		Times Sick	0.285
		Siblings	−0.237
		Career Type	−0.235
2. Military Discipline	11.5	Military Discipline	
		Military Record	
3. Older, Married Stable	9.9	Marital Status	0.838
		Children	0.717
		Residences	0.630
		Age	0.474
		Debts	0.375
4. Criminal History	8.1	Violent Offenses	0.763
		Arrest History	0.611
5. Civilian Complaints	6.6	Civilian Complaints	0.872
		Total Complaints	0.608
6. Harassment	5.7	Harassment	0.706
		Departmental Charges	0.317
		Precinct Hazard	−0.303
7. Education	5.5	Education	0.898
		Last Occupation	0.324
		Background Rating	0.304
		Siblings	0.219

formance characteristics identified in the factor analysis. These differ for the white and black officers.

1. Officers in the 1957 cohort who were most likely to be a discipline problem for the Department, with a large number of Department Charges and Times Sick had the following characteristics:

Whites	Blacks
Young at time of appointment	High I.Q.
Non-college graduate	Few siblings
Excessive summonses and debts	Poor background rating
Employment disciplinary record	Low recruit score
Poor background rating	Poor probationary evaluation
Low recruit training score	Born in New York City
Poor probationary evaluation	

2. Officers most likely to incur charges of Harassment (false arrest, protested summons, illegal search, illegal detention, etc.) had the following characteristics:

Whites	Blacks
No history of prior arrest	No history of prior arrest
History of civil court appearances	Employment disciplinary record
Military disciplinary record	

3. Officers most likely to incur civilian complaints had the following characteristics:

Whites	Blacks
Young at time of appointment	Low I.Q.
Non-college graduate	Many appearances in civil court
Military disciplinary record	Military disciplinary record

4. Men most likely to win many police department awards and commendations had the following characteristics:

Whites	Blacks
Served in military	Marksman
High recruit training score	
Excessive summonses	
High I.Q.	
Marksman	

5. Men who were college graduates at time of appointment or who obtained a college degree while on the force had the following performance characteristics:

Likely to be promoted to sergeant, lieutenant, or captain
Low incidence of misconduct: departmental, criminal, civilian complaints, and harassment
Low sick time, fewer injury disapprovals
Unlikely to have removal of firearms
Low number of awards.

Police Career Profiles

There are two major routes for career advancement in the New York City Police Department: civil service promotions and detective appointments.

Civil service promotions lead to the ranks of sergeant, lieutenant, and captain and require examinations. Appointments above the rank of captain (e.g., Deputy Inspector, Inspector, Deputy Chief Inspector, etc.) are made at the discretion of the Police Commissioner. The detective selection system runs parallel to the promotion route and includes three grades of detective: third grade, second grade, and first grade. There is no examination required for detective appointments or promotions. Instead, the Office of the Chief of Detectives with some assistance from the Police Personnel Bureau selects men for the Division who are then officially appointed by the Police Commissioner. The profiles of detectives and uniformed supervisors are presented below.

Detectives	*Sergeants, Lieutenants, and Captains*
Older at appointment	Younger at appointment
Men with average I.Q.	Men with high I.Q.s
More likely to be married	More likely to be single
Not college educated	College educated
Lower civil service scores	Higher civil service scores
Lower recruit training scores	Higher recruit training scores
Less likely to be an expert marksman	More likely to be an expert marksman

7

Conclusions and Recommendations

Conclusions

A major conclusion of this study is that data commonly maintained in personnel files by police departments can be summarized in terms of a small number of distinct aspects of job performance that are related to another small collection of important predictor variables. Although the nature of the relationships between these predictors and dimensions of performance are not identical for black and white officers, the same variables proved to be important for both races. This finding suggests that it is not necessary to adopt separate selection procedures for white and black officers. Regrettably, there were not enough Hispanic officers in our cohort to analyze their performance patterns separately from those of the other officers.

In the absence of supervisory evaluations in the files for the cohort of officers appointed in 1957, only the following dimensions of performance could be identified and related to predictor variables:

1. *termination*, which describes the officer who left the Department prior to 1968, either voluntarily or involuntarily;
2. *career advancement*, which refers to the officer who obtained special assignments or promotions, frequently coupled with above-average numbers of awards;
3. *departmental discipline problem*, which describes the officer who had an above-average number of departmental charges, and frequently also had an above-average number of times sick;
4. above-average number of *civilian complaints*; and
5. above-average number of allegations of *harassment*.

A fairly substantial group of officers, numbering in the hundreds, displays none of these patterns. The men in this group remained on patrol for eleven years, obtained average or below-average numbers of awards, and did not present any special discipline problems. Presumably, departments that obtain supervisory evaluations of performance based on field activities would find they could distinguish effective from ineffective officers within this group. Subsequent to the completion of the present study, the New York Police Department implemented such a system of performance evaluations.

We found for the white subjects that many of the traditional "negative"

121

indicators of past performance were indeed predictors of at least one of the dimensions of ineffective performance. For example, military discipline and employment discipline record were found to be consistent predictors of the pattern of the departmental discipline problem. Moreover, multiple appearances in civil court were the strongest predictor of the harassment pattern, although differences between officers with and without multiple court appearances were not large. We therefore have some indication that a history of court appearances may in fact reflect difficulty in getting along with people. Other factors that are usually viewed as negative and that may also be related to a pattern of ineffective performance, although the data were not conclusive on these, were arrests for violent crimes, multiple summonses, and debts.

Among the black officers, the only negative factor that attained significance as a predictor in a regression equation was civil court appearances, which was found to be related to above-average civilian complaints. In addition, an employment disciplinary record and military discipline were generally associated with ineffective performance for blacks, although they did not appear as significant predictors in any of the regression equations.

In one instance, a so-called "negative" indicator was actually associated with effective performance. White officers with a prior arrest (not for a violent crime) were found to have lower incidence of the harassment pattern. On the other hand, high I.Q., traditionally viewed as a positive attribute, was found to be related to a higher incidence of departmental discipline problems among black officers. The same was not true of white officers with high I.Q., who appeared to be generally effective performers and in particular had above-average awards and attained promoted ranks.

Clearly, the implication of this is not that police departments should refuse to accept black applicants with high I.Q. Rather, it suggests that the New York Police Department may not be currently meeting the needs of its most intelligent black recruits. Among the intelligent white applicants, we found that a disproportionate number left the Department (this was identified from the termination rates of officers with higher education). For the blacks who found themselves similarly unsuited for police work, the options in other occupations may not have been as attractive for them as for whites in the late 1950s, and therefore they remained as somewhat unsatisfied and unsatisfactory officers.

If police departments wish to attract and retain more intelligent and more educated officers, they will have to recognize that these men may not be suitable for certain assignments, and they may not be satisfied with the long periods required to attain promotions or with other aspects of the department's operations. These officers should be given special attention by police administrators. The similarity of our finding in regard to early termination by college-educated officers to findings in other cities suggests the need for a questionnaire-interview study of a sample of intelligent, educated officers who either left police work or failed to attain satisfactory performance, in order to determine the source of their discontent. Police departments might then be able to plan new procedures and incentive systems that will improve the retention and performance of such officers, especially in their early years. One possibility is that the starting salary of recruits could be determined in accordance with their level of education. Such a procedure would be entirely consistent with the principle that compensation should be related to performance, since we found that college-educated officers in New York performed at a level well above average.[a]

We might also note that, although men who obtain college degrees while on the force appear to be excellent performers, this does not necessarily suggest that all men would improve their performance if they attended college. We are no doubt observing a combination of motivation, stamina, and intelligence in the men who completed college. The Department should evidently encourage and assist in every way possible officers who wish to advance their education. However, it appears to us that the New York Police Department will continue to need officers of average I.Q. and no college education. For example, our finding that the members of our cohort who remained in the Traffic Division predominantly had these characteristics suggests that these men are good performers in traffic duty. Probably, if more educated recruits were given traffic assignments, they would be dissatisfied with the lack of challenge of their job and their inability to apply what they have learned in college. On the other hand, we found that the older and more educated subjects were less likely to incur civilian complaints than their younger, less educated counterparts. This suggests that older officers with advanced education should be assigned on a permanent basis to sensitive areas in greater numbers, and also they should make up the units that are routinely mobilized and assigned to trouble spots.

We find that in New York the Police Department's background investigators are fairly skillful at weighing together all of an applicant's characteristics and deriving an overall appraisal. In general, the men they rated "excellent" turned out to be well above average, and many of those termed "poor" or "disapproved" were later found to be departmental discipline problems. This suggests that the recommendations of the background investigator be given considerable weight in accepting candidates. There may, however, be some danger of decreasing the number of minority group members among appointees with a procedure that allows the investigators to reject a larger fraction of applicants than they have in the past. Our data showed that the ratings of blacks tended to be lower in general than those of whites and that more background characteristics were found to correlate negatively with background ratings for blacks than for whites.[b] This occurred in spite of the fact that

[a]We are indebted to Marvin E. Wolfgang for suggesting this possibility after reading an early draft of this study.

[b]In the 1969 Hunt and Cohen study[46] on minority recruiting, there was some evidence supporting the objectivity of the present background investigators, since discrimination by race did not appear to enter as a factor in their overall evaluation to accept or reject a candidate.

the blacks were better educated than the whites and did not differ from the whites on any aspect of military or employment history, arrest or summons history, or the number of times they had appeared in civil court.

We believe this difficulty can be overcome by assigning an adequate number of black and Hispanic officers to investigate the backgrounds of candidates, and by instructing the investigators as to the findings of this study about characteristics that were and were not related to later performance. Marginal candidates should be reviewed by investigators of like background and ethnicity. On balance, we would trust the background investigators to produce an overall appraisal of each candidate from the data contained in the application form, using the findings of the present study as a guide.

A very important finding of this study is that the strongest predictors of later performance are obtained after the candidate has been accepted as a recruit. These include his recruit training score and his probationary education. This suggests that the New York Police Department should consider developing an extensive program of evaluating the performance of recruits and terminating the services of much larger numbers than has ever been done in the past. In 1957, less than 1 percent of the recruits were dropped from the academy or during probation. The fraction has not been substantially higher in recent years in New York, and is probably typical of many cities. We feel that the benefits to the community in terms of improving police service and avoiding the expense of salaries and retirement benefits for unsatisfactory policemen clearly outweigh the disadvantages of possible false rejection of men who perform poorly in their first year on the force but might improve later.

Our data showed that low scores in recruit training and probationary evaluation, taken together, were good predictors of future unsatisfactory career advancement, departmental misconduct brought to trial and substantiated, and a low history of awards. Rather than taking the attitude that men who do poorly in the police academy or on probation should be given a second chance, we feel that the Police Commissioner should use the option available to him under the civil service laws to terminate the services of such recruits. For this purpose, a special review board could be established to consider carefully the record of each officer at the end of his probationary period and to recommend action to the Police Commissioner in each instance. If a recruit's background investigation rating was marginal, but he was accepted for the probationary period anyway, this should be taken into account at the same time, in light of his probationary performance.

In 1957, there was a small number of men (20) who had two unsatisfactory marks on probation and also scored below average in the Police Academy. The records of these men were found to be uniformly worse than average on all aspects of performance. Therefore, our findings suggest that such men could be separated from the force at the end of the probationary period with little risk of losing officers who would perform well later in their careers.

Some factors were not found to be related in important ways to our performance measures, for those who were accepted by the Department and remained on the force. For the whites, these were I.Q.; grade on civil service exam beyond passing; presence of a family mental disorder; region of birth; number of siblings; father's occupation; applicant's number of jobs and last occupation; military service; military commendations; number of residences; aspects of early family responsibility, including marital status, number of children, and debts; reported history of psychological disorder; and number of summonses. For the black officers, the data suggest removing region of birth and number of siblings from this list, but it is not clear that such information should actually be used in selecting candidates. We could not determine the relationship for black subjects between the following background factors and performance measures because of insufficient data: family mental disorder, psychological disorder, education, and an arrest for a violent offense.

When all factors are taken into account, it appears that the strongest predictors for subjects of both races are those quantifiable measures that reflect the subject's primary behavior and experience over a period of time, such as education, repeated civil court appearances, an employment disciplinary record, military discipline, recruit training score, and probationary rating, rather than factors which tend to label or stigmatize persons as good or bad (e.g., history of a petty crime, I.Q., etc.).

Nearly all aspects of performance that we were able to measure in this study were found to be predictable from background characteristics. For the white officers, they include, in order of predictive validity, career type, substantiated complaints, trials, departmental charges, absenteeism, total complaints, awards, civilian complaints, and harassment. Only relationships between background factors and criminal complaints, removal of firearms for cause, and invalid claims of injury failed to attain statistical significance in the regression equations. A possible explanation for the absence of predictive validity are that there were too few officers with these characteristics to establish statistical significance. In this study, we did not use psychological tests as predictors, and these may be required to predict such aspects of performance as the removal of firearms for cause.

Among the black subjects, four aspects of performance were predictable. They are, in order of amenability of prediction, trials, career type, civilian complaints, and departmental charges. Thus, for black as well as white officers, different forms of misconduct, one involving violation of departmental norms and the other complaints by civilians, may be predicted by background factors.

The general performance measures that we developed could not be validly predicted for both the white and the black officers. We therefore cannot suggest a uniform method of scoring the background and early performance measures to obtain an overall rating. However, a low rating on both probationary evaluation and recruit training score should be considered as more negative than a low score on only one of these measures.

The background factors used in this study were unable to predict performance for the subgroup consisting of detectives. One plausible explanation for the absence of predictive validity for performance of detectives is that promotion of detectives within the Detective Division depends less on standards of performance than on other factors such as seniority or happenstance of who may be in position to influence appointments at any given time. Our findings that individual performance measures were amenable to prediction for the total active cohort and also certain subgroups (e.g., black officers) that were even smaller in size than the subgroup of detectives supports our notion that both background factors and recruitment factors discriminate among subjects when actual performance differs.

* * *

Because findings and conclusions of the type described here have been found to vary when conducted in other police departments or at other times, we would not wish to see our results applied as if they had universal validity. However, the methods we used could be readily adapted to the personnel files of nearly any police department in the country, and further research along these lines, including validation studies, would indicate the extent to which the New York City 1957 cohort shows typical patterns of relationships between background characteristics and performance.

Recommendations

Although this work was undertaken with a view to obtaining findings of interest to police departments across the country, inevitably we were led to certain observations specific to the New York City Police Department, the source of our data. The recommendations that we presented to the Department, based on these observations, are given below. In subsequent work for the Department, we are assisting in the implementation of some of them.

1. Although many differences in detail were found between the patterns of background variables vs. performance variables for whites and the patterns for blacks, on balance the major implications for police selection were similar for both races. We therefore recommend as practical and feasible a single selection procedure, as described below, to be applied to all applicants without regard to race.

   (a) In the current procedure, all candidates who qualify for appointment in regard to statutory and medical requirements are reviewed by Police Department background investigators. This part of the appointment process should certainly be retained. Although we have no way of knowing what performance levels could be expected from men who fail the civil service examination for patrolman, there is no indication from the data that men who pass but score low on this exam are any less satisfactory than men who score high. Therefore, the findings of this study are not conclusive in regard to the effectiveness of the exam as currently used in the appointment process, and they do not suggest how the passing grade should be established. Considerations beyond those addressed in this study apply to the use of a civil service examination. For example, at the very least, it weeds out many applicants who are not serious enough about becoming policemen to show up at an examination center, and it has traditionally been viewed as a method of preventing favoritism from influencing municipal appointments.

(b) We propose that the background investigators provide their overall rating of each applicant's suitability for appointment after taking into account the findings of this study as to the significance of various aspects and characteristics of background.

(c) Potential discrimination by race in this procedure, which might have been a factor in 1957 but has not been proved to exist currently in the New York City Police Department by any data known to us, should be avoidable by assigning a sufficient number of black and Hispanic investigators to review the backgrounds of candidates. These investigators could help interpret the characteristics of candidates of like ethnicity and background when there is a question of acceptance.

(d) No candidate should be discouraged from continuing his application on the basis of missing or "negative" information in any of the categories, such as prior arrest for nonviolent crime, absence of military commendations or military service, etc., which this study found did not predict later bad performance. We feel that the candidate hearing boards, which review the decisions of background investigators, are a useful part of the selection process, because although the investigators' ratings have predictive validity, mistakes are nonetheless made.

(e) Finally, an extensive program should be developed for evaluating the performance of recruits. Recruits who perform poorly should be terminated in much larger numbers than has ever been done in the past, based on low grades in the Police Academy and unsatisfactory probationary evaluation. Low grades on both of these measures should be considered as more negative than a low score on any one of them. However, the potential effects of an increased rate of dismissing probationary patrolmen on the morale of recruits and on the type of candidate who applies to the Department should also be considered carefully before beginning such a program.

2. Since men who obtained college degrees either prior to or after joining the force were good performers, the Department should attempt to attract and retain such men and should assist them in continuing their education. However, we believe that men of average intelligence and no college education are still

needed in substantial numbers for assignments such as traffic duty, where they appear to perform well and become stable, satisfied employees.

3. Officers who are older at time of appointment and have advanced education should be assigned in greater numbers on a permanent basis to sensitive areas of the City, and also they should be heavily represented in those units which are routinely mobilized and assigned to trouble spots. This is a direct result of our finding that the older and more educated subjects were less likely to incur civilian complaints than their younger, less educated counterparts.

4. The Police Department should broaden the parts of the Police Academy training program which are aimed at improving police performance during police-citizen transactions. Similar refresher courses should also be designed and required of officers already on the force. The need for expanding programs of this kind is indicated by the fact that officers' performance in the Academy training program was a strong predictor of internal departmental performance measures such as career advancement, departmental disciplinary actions, and absenteeism, but it was not predictive of those aspects of behavior that generally involve police interactions with citizens, such as civilian complaints. In addition, the finding that officers with a prior arrest for a petty crime had statistically fewer complaints of harassment suggests the need for additional courses such as those involving role-playing, in which recruits would be subjected to the experience of being "arrested."

5. Although our research led to a number of separate performance measures, most of them reflect a departmental, rather than a community, view of officers' performance. We urge that the Department devise additional measures, particularly positive ones based upon field activities and taking into account police-community transactions. Admittedly, this is a difficult task, but the benefits to both the community and the Department in terms of increased police performance and effectiveness make this work essential.

6. A computer-based information system for police performance data should be developed, incorporating the pieces of data on performance found to be important in the present study. Most of this information is currently collected by separate units in the Police Department, but in its present form it is virtually useless. The proposed data system would integrate the relevant pieces of information having predictive value and provide a data base for computing general performance scores for each officer.

7. Available measures of performance of detectives proved not to be predictable, suggesting that the measures themselves are not satisfactory indicators of actual performance. We therefore support the Department's efforts to develop new criteria for selection and promotion of detectives.

Appendices

Appendix A: Data Coding Sheets

Name _____   Tax No. _____

Iden. _____

SUBJECT CARD

Identification	☐☐☐☐	No. of Debts	☐
Continuation	☐	Father's Occup.	☐
Year of Birth	☐☐	No. of Siblings	☐
Region of Birth	☐	No. of Fam. Arrests	☐
Race	☐	Other Arrests (No.)	☐
No. of Residences	☐☐	Background Investigation	☐
No. of Yrs. in N.Y.		Reason	☐☐
Prior to Appointment	☐		
Present Residence	☐	Total No. of Charges	☐☐
Relationship	☐	Year of 1st Charge	☐☐
Criminal History (No.)	☐	Type	☐☐
Charge	☐	Disposition	☐
Adult-Juvenile Status	☐	Year of 2nd Charge	☐☐
Disposition	☐	Type	☐☐
Charge	☐	Disposition	☐
Adult-Juvenile Status	☐	Year of 3rd Charge	☐☐
Disposition	☐	Type	☐☐
No. of Summonses	☐	Disposition	☐
No. Complaints (Court)	☐	Year of 4th Charge	☐☐
No. Family Mental		Type	☐☐
Health	☐	Disposition	☐
Relationship	☐	Total No. of Awards	☐☐
Educational Att.	☐	Year of 1st Award	☐☐
No. of Jobs	☐☐	Type	☐
Last Occupation	☐☐	Year of 2nd Award	☐☐
No. Empl. Disc. Record	☐	Type	☐
Marital Status	☐	Year of 3rd Award	☐☐
No. of Children	☐	Type	☐
Paternity Proceedings	☐	Year of 4th Award	☐☐
Military Record	☐	Type	☐
Military Disc. Rec.	☐		

Name _____   Tax No. _____

Iden. _____

FORCE CARD

Identification	☐☐☐☐	Precinct Last Assignment	45 ☐☐☐
Continuation	5 2	Duty (last)	☐
Current Rank	☐☐	Hazard Status (last)	☐
Current Dept. Status	8 ☐	First Promotion (Rank)	50 ☐
Date of Termination	Mo. Yr. ☐☐ ☐☐	Date	Mo. Yr. ☐☐ ☐☐
Total Number of Assignments (or Transfers)	☐☐	Second Promotion (Rank)	55 ☐
Precinct First Assignment	15 ☐☐☐	Date	Mo. Yr. ☐☐ ☐☐
Date	Mo. Yr. ☐☐ ☐☐	Third Promotion (Rank)	60 ☐
Duty (1st)	22 ☐	Date	Mo. Yr. ☐☐ ☐☐
Hazard Status (1st)	☐	Fourth Promotion (Rank)	65 ☐
Precinct Second Assignment	26 ☐☐☐	Date	Mo. Yr. ☐☐ ☐☐
Date	Mo. Yr. ☐☐ ☐☐	Current Social Condition	70 ☐
Duty (2nd)	☐	Date	Mo. Yr. ☐☐ ☐☐
Hazard Status (2nd)	☐	Current Residence	☐
Third Assignment (Hazard Status)	33 ☐	Recruit Training Score	77 ☐☐
Date	Mo. Yr. ☐☐ ☐☐	Highest Educational Attainment	☐
Duty (3rd)	☐		
Fourth Assignment (Hazard Status)	39 ☐	Major Status	☐
Date	Mo. Yr. ☐☐ ☐☐		80 ☐
Duty (4th)	☐		

Name _____   Tax No. _____

Iden. _____

MEDICAL CARD

Identification	4 ☐☐☐☐	Rank (2nd N.F.A.)	50 ☐☐
Continuation	③	No. Mo. Bet. 1st & 2nd (N.F.A.)	☐☐
Current Status	☐	No. Injury Disapprovals	☐
Total Times Sick	☐☐	Alcohol	54 ☐
Total No. of Days Sick (Ld)	10 ☐☐☐	Date	Mo. Yr. ☐☐ ☐☐
Total No. of Days Sick (N.Ld)	14 ☐☐☐	Command	☐
Total No. of Days Sick	17 ☐☐☐	I.Q.	60 ☐☐☐
Date 1st Sick Report	Mo. Yr. ☐☐ ☐☐	L.D.S. (No.)	☐
Date 2nd Sick Report	Mo. Yr. ☐☐ ☐☐	Precinct (or Duty)	66 ☐☐☐
Date 3rd Sick Report	Mo. Yr. ☐☐ ☐☐	Residence	☐
Date 4th Sick Report	Mo. Yr. ☐☐ ☐☐	Date Assig. Lds	Mo. Yr. ☐☐ ☐☐
NFA (Number)	34 ☐	Date Terminated	Mo. Yr. ☐☐ ☐☐
Rank (1st)	☐☐	Reason (Lds)	76 ☐☐
Comm'd. Assig. When N.F.A.	1st ☐	LOD	☐
Date Firearms Removed (1st)	Mo. Yr. ☐☐ ☐☐	Month of Appointment	80 ☐☐
Reason (1st)	42 ☐☐		
Duty Status	☐		
Date Restored	Mo. Yr. ☐☐ ☐☐		

Name ———————————————   Tax Number ————

Ident.: ——————————

DETECTIVE CARD

Identification	⁴ ☐☐☐☐	Felony	☐☐☐
Continuation	⁵ ☐(4)	Misdemeanor	³⁵ ☐☐☐
Date	Mo. ☐☐ Yr. ☐☐	Complaints	☐
Command	¹⁰ ☐☐☐		———————————
Age	☐☐	Arrest Activity (Total)	⁴⁰ ☐☐☐
Debts (No.)	¹⁵ ☐	Felonies	☐☐☐
No. of Children	☐	Misdemeanors	⁴⁵ ☐☐☐
Relatives (No.)	☐	Evaluation	☐☐
Rank (of Above)	☐		———————————
Education	²⁰ ☐☐	Approval	⁵⁰ ☐
Promotion Exam (1st)	☐	Reason	⁵² ☐☐
Score	☐☐☐		☐☐
Promotion Exam (2nd)	²⁵ ☐		⁵⁵ ☐☐
Score	☐☐☐		☐☐
Total Arrests	³⁰ ☐☐☐		☐
			⁶⁰ ☐

Name _____   Tax No. _____

Iden. _____

CIVILIAN COMPLAINT CARD

Ident.	☐☐☐☐	☐
	5	60
Continuation	⑤	☐☐
Number of Compl.	☐	☐
Age of Complainant (1st)	☐☐	☐☐
	10	65
(2nd)	☐☐	☐
(3rd)	☐☐	
	Male Female	
Sex	☐ ☐	
	Negro White P.R. or H.	
Race	☐ ☐ ☐	
	Mo. Day Yr.	
Date of Complaint	☐☐ ☐ ☐☐	
	23	
Time of Complaint	☐	
Complain. Arrested	☐	
	25	
Charge	☐	
	Mo. Day Yr.	
Date of Incident	☐☐ ☐ ☐☐	
	31	
Disposition	☐	
No. of Pol. Off.	☐	
	35	
Command (1)	☐☐☐	
Command (2)	☐☐☐	
	40	
Command (3)	☐☐☐	
Years on Force (1)	☐☐	
	45	
Years on Force (2)	☐☐	
Years on Force (3)	☐☐	
	Negro White P.R. or H.	
Race	☐ ☐ ☐	
	51	
Complaint Category	☐	
Substantiated	☐	
Recommendation	☐☐	
	55	
Col.	☐	
Precinct (of Complaint)	☐☐☐	

Address _____

Occupation _____

Name _____   Tax Number _____

Iden. _____

CIIU – PM – FDC

Iden.	⁴ ☐☐☐☐	Alleged	⁴⁶ ☐
Continuation	⁶ ☒	Disposition	☐☐
Charge (1)	☐☐	Formal Charges	⁴⁹ ☐
Unit	⁸ ☐	Plainclothes	⁵⁰ ☐
Date	Mo. Yr. ☐☐ ☐☐	Date of Appointment	Mo. Yr. ☐☐ ☐☐
Alleged	¹³ ☐	Date of Termination	Mo. Yr. ☐☐ ☐☐
Disposition	¹⁵ ☐☐		⁵⁹ ☐
Formal Charges	☐		⁶⁰ ☐☐
Charge (2)	☐☐		☐☐ ⁶⁵ ☐☐
Unit	¹⁹ ☐		☐
Date	Mo. Yr. ☐☐ ☐☐		☐
Alleged	☐		☐☐
Disposition	²⁵ ☐☐		⁷⁰ ☐☐ ☐☐
Formal Charges	☐		⁷⁴ ☐
Charge (3)	☐☐		
Unit	³⁰ ☐		
Date	Mo. Yr. ☐☐ ☐☐		
Alleged	³⁵ ☐		
Disposition	☐☐		
Formal Charges	☐		
Charge (4)	⁴⁰ ☐☐	Code No. (1st):	
Unit	☐	(2nd):	
Date	Mo. Yr. ☐☐ ☐☐	(3rd):	

Appendix B: Police Department Forms

P.A.1
Evaluation of   **POLICE DEPARTMENT**   Date of
Probationer   City of New York   Appointment _____

——————————————— ——————— ——————— ————Precinct
(Surname) (First Name) (Initial) Shield Number Company Number Field Command
     Probationary Patrolman

PART I

Official Instructor		S	U*
Intellectual	1. Capacity		
Qualities	2. Knowledge		
	3. Written Expression		
	4. Oral Expression		
Social	5. Appearance-Bearing		
Adaptability	6. Manner-Amenity		
	7. Tact-Patience		
Career	8. Interest-Industry		
Mindedness	9. Attitude-Ethics		
Physical	10. Physical Training		
	11. First Aid		
Firearms	12. Qualification		

PART II

Field Commander		S	U*
Perform-	13. Law Enforcement		
ance	14. Attitude towards Public		
Factors	15. Attention to Duty		
	16. Report Writing		
	17. Follow Directions		
Personal	18. Respect for Authority		
Traits	19. Interest in Career		
	20. Resourcefulness		
	21. Trustworthiness		
	22. Teamwork-Cooperation		
KEY: S – Satisfactory U – Unsatisfactory			

Each of the Above Factors Must be Check-Marked by the Superior Concerned

PART III

	Police* Academy	Field* Command
Unsatisfactory Incidents		
Emotional Instability: Too sensitive, too easily frustrated? Unsteady under pressure, unreliable, or erratic under emergency conditions?		
Poor Judgment: Lacks common sense? Acts without thinking? Draws unreasonable conclusions? Makes premature snap decisions?		
Undesirable Aggressiveness: Has chip on his shoulder? Acts belligerently, abusively? Takes advantage of his authority?		
Intemperance: Evidence of over-indulgence in liquor? Evidence of immoderation in any other pursuits?		
Unwillingness to Cooperate: Reluctant to do his share? Waits to be ordered, neglects to do his work unless supervised?		
Extreme Introvert-Extrovert: Moody, unfriendly? Talks too much, interferes in the affairs of others? Unreasonably imposes his opinions?		
Lack of Self-Confidence: Lacks called-for decisiveness? Fails to assume his proper responsibility? Overly timid?		
Other Undesirable Manifestations: any other undesirable traits which may render him unsuitable for police service?		

PART III AND PART IV — These items will be checked in appropriate cases only.

PART IV

		Police* Academy	Field* Command
Accomplishments	Arrests		
	Rescues		
	Other Commendatory Action		
Disciplinary	Department Charges		
Actions	Civilian Complaints		
	Academy Delinquencies–Precinct Reprimands		

(continued)

Official Instructor	My evaluation of the Probationer is: Satisfactory Unsatisfactory
	Lt. Sgt. _____ Date_____
Commanding Officer, Police Academy	Recommend: Immediate Termination of Services Continuance of Probation
	_____ Date_____
Field Commander	Recommend: Permanent Appointment Termination of Services
	Capt. _____ Date_____

*Explanatory Report Required.   (Reverse side for instructions)

_____

EVALUATION REPORT – DETECTIVES

Surname	First Name	MI	Gr.- Sh. #	Command	Date Assigned to Command

Tax Registry No.	Type of Duty Performed	Rating Period From To

Date Appointed to

PD	DD	D-3	D-2	D-1

Special Duty Assignments:			Sick Report:	
Year	No of Days	Duty Assignment and Command	No of Days	Nature of Illness

Arrest Activity

Year	Felonies	Misdemeanors	Miscellaneous
Totals			

Note: All raters should be aware of the serious responsibility imposed upon them to report objectively, fairly and without prejudice. Consider each factor carefully for every member rated.   (continued)

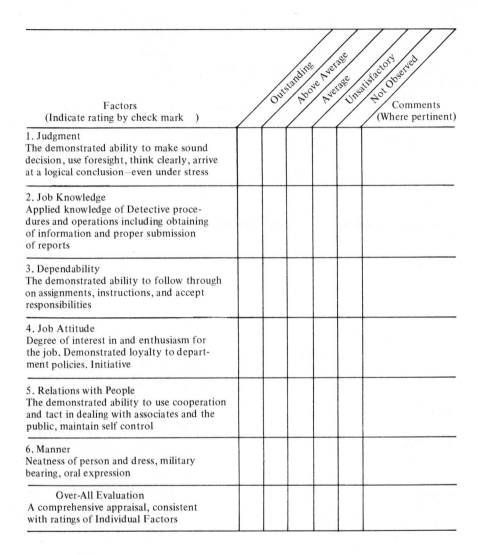

Factors (Indicate rating by check mark)	Outstanding	Above Average	Average	Unsatisfactory	Not Observed	Comments (Where pertinent)
1. Judgment The demonstrated ability to make sound decision, use foresight, think clearly, arrive at a logical conclusion—even under stress						
2. Job Knowledge Applied knowledge of Detective procedures and operations including obtaining of information and proper submission of reports						
3. Dependability The demonstrated ability to follow through on assignments, instructions, and accept responsibilities						
4. Job Attitude Degree of interest in and enthusiasm for the job. Demonstrated loyalty to department policies. Initiative						
5. Relations with People The demonstrated ability to use cooperation and tact in dealing with associates and the public, maintain self control						
6. Manner Neatness of person and dress, military bearing, oral expression						
Over-All Evaluation A comprehensive appraisal, consistent with ratings of Individual Factors						

Appendix C: Variables Suppressed in Regression Equations

In some of the regression analyses, one or more of the background variables were found not to enter the regression equation with significance at the .05 level due to the prior introduction of another background variable. We call the missing variables "suppressed" variables, and the variable which replaced them the "suppressor." Since the multiple correlation would have been almost as high if one of the suppressed variables had entered instead of the suppressor, a listing of the suppressed variable may be of interest to police departments which lack some of the data used in this study. This listing is given in Table C-1.

To interpret the table, one should note that at each step in the multiple regression analysis, the independent variable having the highest F statistic is entered next. If another variable has a slightly lower F statistic and is correlated with the variable entered, its value of F will decrease when the variable is entered, and it is thereby suppressed. The first value of F noted on Table C-1 is

Table C-1
Suppressed Variables in Regressions

Total Active Cohort				
Dependent Variable	Suppressed Variable	F	Suppressor Variable	F
Career Type	I.Q.	21.22	Civil Service	34.16
	Education	11.35	Civil Service	
Total Complaints	Background Rating	4.58	Military Disc.	4.99
Substantiated Complaints	Background Rating	8.61	Military Disc.	10.14
Departmental Charges	Military Disc.	5.39	Background Rating	12.43
	Jobs	4.63	Employ. Disc.	4.70
Times Sick	Military Disc.	4.57	Background Rating	4.79
General Performance Index	I.Q.	8.56	Civil Service	12.14

Black Actives				
Dependent Variable	Suppressed Variable	F	Suppressor Variable	F
Trials	Unsatisfactory Probation	4.28	I.Q.	4.41

143

the *F* which the suppressed variable would have had if entered into the regression equation instead of the suppressor. The second value of *F* corresponds to the variable actually entered in the regression. The following are the cutoff levels for significance at the .05 level: for the total cohort, $F = 6.63$; for the black actives, $F = 4.00$.

Bibliography

Bibliography

1. THE CHALLENGE OF CRIME IN A FREE SOCIETY: A REPORT BY THE PRESIDENT'S COMMISSION ON LAW ENFORCEMENT AND ADMINISTRATION OF JUSTICE, U.S. Government Printing Office, Washington, D.C., 1967, Chapter IV; REPORT OF THE NATIONAL ADVISORY COMMISSION ON CIVIL DISORDERS, Bantam Books, Inc., New York, 1968, Chapter II; TO ESTABLISH JUSTICE, TO INSURE DOMESTIC TRANQUILITY: FINAL REPORT OF THE NATIONAL COMMISSION ON THE CAUSES AND PREVENTION OF VIOLENCE, U.S. Government Printing Office, Washington, D.C., 1969, Chapter 3, para. 76, and Appendix 1, para. 275.
2. Singer, George, MORALE FACTORS IN INDUSTRIAL MANAGEMENT, Exposition Press, New York, 1961.
3. Kates, Solis L., "Rorschach Responses, Strong Blank Scales, and Job Satisfaction Among Policemen," J. APPL. PSYCH., Vol. 34, 1950, pp. 249-54.
4. Baehr, Melany E., John E. Furcon, and Ernest C. Froemel, "Psychological Assessment of Patrolman Qualifications in Relation to Field Performance," The Industrial Relations Center, University of Chicago, 1968. Available from the Superintendent of Documents, U.S. Government Printing Office, Washington, D.C.
5. Blum, Richard M. (ed.), POLICE SELECTION, Charles C. Thomas, Springfield, Illinois, 1964, pp. 123-134.
6. Collins, Jack G., "A Study of the Use of the Humm-Wadsworth Temperament Scale by the Los Angeles Police Department," unpublished Master's thesis, School of Public Administration, University of Southern California, 1965.
7. Colarelli, Nick J., and Saul M. Siegel, "A Method of Police Personnel Selection," THE JOURNAL OF CRIMINAL LAW, CRIMINOLOGY, AND POLICE SCIENCE, Vol. 55, 1964, pp. 287-89.
8. Cross, Arthur C., and Kenneth R. Hammond, "Social Differences between 'Successful' and 'Unsuccessful' State Highway Patrolmen," PUBL. PERS. REV., Vol. 11, 1951, p. 33.
9. DuBois, Philip H., and Robert I. Watson, "The Selection of Patrolmen," J. APPL. PSYCH., Vol. 34, 1950, pp. 90-95.
10. Dubois, Philip H., "Long Range Prediction of Police Criteria," unpublished report for the Board of Police Commissioners, St. Louis, Missouri, 1962.
11. Eilbert, Leo R., "Research on the Selection of Police Recruits," unpublished report of the American Institute for Research, 1966.
12. Hankey, Richard O., "Personality Correlates in a Role of Authority: The Police," unpublished D.P.A. dissertation, University of Southern California, 1968.

13. Hogan, Robert, "A Study of Police Effectiveness," Experimental Publication System, AMERICAN PSYCHOLOGICAL ASSOCIATION, Washington, D.C., June 1970.

14. Humm, Doncaster G., and Kathryn A. Humm, "Humm-Wadsworth Temperament Scale Appraisals Compared with Criteria of Job Success in the Los Angeles Police Department," JOUR. PSYCH., Vol. 30, 1950, pp. 63-75.

15. Levy, Ruth, "Summary of Report on Retrospective Study of 5,000 Peace Officer Personnel Records," THE POLICE YEARBOOK, International Association of Chiefs of Police, 1966, pp. 61-63.

16. _____, "Predicting Police Failures," THE JOURNAL OF CRIMINAL LAW, CRIMINOLOGY AND POLICE SCIENCE, Vol. 58, 1967, pp. 265-276.

17. Marsh, Stewart H., "Validating the Selection of Deputy Sheriffs," PUBL. PERSONNEL REV., Vol. 23, 1962, pp. 41-44.

18. McAllister, John A., "A Study of the Prediction and Measurement of Police Performance," unpublished M.P.A. thesis, John Jay College of Criminal Justice, City University of New York, 1968.

19. Mullineaux, Jewel E., "An Evaluation of the Predictors Used to Select Patrolmen," PUBL. PERSONNEL REV., Vol. 16, pp. 84-86.

20. Spencer, Gilmore, and Robert Nichols, "A Study of Chicago Police Recruits: Validation of Selection Procedures," THE POLICE CHIEF, Vol. 38, No. 6, June, 1971, pp. 50-55.

21. Valla, F. Louis, "Predicting Tenure of Border Patrol Inspectors," PERSONNEL ADMIN., Vol. 22, 1959, pp. 27-29.

22. Abbatiello, A., "A Study of Police Candidate Selection," Paper Presented at the Seventy-Seventh Annual Convention of the American Psychological Association, Washington, D.C., 1969.

23. Chwast, Jacob, "Selection of Personnel for a Police Juvenile Service," THE JOURNAL OF CRIMINAL LAW, CRIMINOLOGY AND POLICE SCIENCE, Vol. 51, 1960, pp. 357-362.

24. Gambol, Ann Marie, Norbert S. Slowikowski, and Chet Doyle, "Detective Selection Gets a New Twist in Chicago," PUBLIC PERSONNEL REVIEW, Vol. 26, 1965, pp. 40-43.

25. McDevit, Robert J., "Situational Tests in Metropolitan Police Selection," THE JOURNAL OF CRIMINAL LAW, CRIMINOLOGY AND POLICE SCIENCE, Vol. 57, 1966, pp. 99-106.

26. Mills, Robert B., Robert J. McDevitt, and Sandra Tonkin, "Situational Tests in Metropolitan Police Recruit Selection," THE JOURNAL OF CRIMINAL LAW, CRIMINOLOGY AND POLICE SCIENCE, Vol. 57, 1966, pp. 99-104.

27. Morman, Robert R., Richard O. Hankey, Harold L. Heywood, and Rogers L. Liddle, "Predicting State Traffic Officer Cadet Academic Performance from Theoretical TAV Selection System Scores," POLICE, Vol. 10, No. 3, 1966, pp. 54-58.

28. Morman, Robert R., Richard O. Hankey, Phyllis K. Kennedy, and Ethel M. Jones, "Academy Achievement of State Traffic Officer Cadets Related to TAV Selection System Plus Other Variables," POLICE, Vol. 10, No. 6, 1966, pp. 30-34.

29. Morman, Robert R., Richard O. Hankey, Harold L. Heywood, Rogers L. Liddle, and Marie Goldwhite, "Multiple Prediction of Municipal Police Officers' Ratings and Rankings Using the Theoretical TAV Selection System and Certain Non-Test Data," POLICE, Vol. 11, No. 3, 1967, pp. 19-22.

30. Newman, James M., William E. Rogin, William K. Hunter, and Shanti Vora, "Investigation of a Method for Identification of the High Risk Police Applicant: An Analysis and Interpretation Based on Available Data," in CAN HIGH-RISK POLICE APPLICANTS BE IDENTIFIED?, Institute for Local Self Government, Berkeley, California, July 1971, pp. 59-89.

31. Siegal, Saul M., "Method of Police Personnel Selections," THE JOURNAL OF CRIMINAL LAW, CRIMINOLOGY AND POLICE SCIENCE, Vol. 55, 1964, pp. 287-194.

32. Tent, Deborah Ann, and Terry Eisenberg, "The Selection and Promotion of Police Officers: A Selected Review of Recent Literature," POLICE CHIEF, Vol. 39, No. 2, February 1972, pp. 20-29.

33. Furcon, John, Ernest C. Froemel, Ronald G. Franczak, and Melany E. Baehr, A LONGITUDINAL STUDY OF PSYCHOLOGICAL TEST PRE-DICTORS AND ASSESSMENTS OF PATROLMAN FIELD PERFORM-ANCE, Report submitted to the National Institute of Law Enforcement and Criminal Justice, Law Enforcement Assistance Administration, June 1, 1971. Available from the Superintendent of Documents, U.S. Government Printing Office, Washington, D.C.

34. Blum, Richard H. (ed.), POLICE SELECTION, Charles E. Thomas, Springfield, Illinois, 1964, 106-107.

35. Wolfgang, Marvin E., Robert Figlio, and Thorsten Sellin, DELINQUENCY IN A BIRTH COHORT, The University of Chicago Press, Chicago, 1972.

36. Duncan, Otis Dudley, "A Socioeconomic Index for All Occupations," Chapter IV and Appendix B in Reiss, Albert J., OCCUPATIONS AND SOCIAL STATUS, The Free Press of Glencoe, Inc., New York, 1961.

37. Blum, Richard H. (ed.), POLICE SELECTION, Charles C. Thomas, Springfield, Illinois, 1964, pp. 109-110.

38. Cohen, Bernard, THE POLICE INTERNAL ADMINISTRATION OF JUS-TICE IN NEW YORK CITY, R-621-NYC, The New York City-Rand Institute, November 1970.

39. Griggs v. Duke Power Company, 401 U.S. 424 (1971).

40. Carter v. Gallagher, 452 F.2d 315 (8 Cir., 1971).

41. NAACP v. Allen, Civil No. 3561-N (M.D. Ala., Feb. 10, 1972).

42. Chance v. Board of Education, 330 F. Supp. 203 (S.D.N.Y., 1971). Affirmed on appeal.

43. Guardians v. Civil Service Commission, Civil Action No. 72-928 (S.D.N.Y., 1972).

44. Blalock, Jr., Hubert M., SOCIAL STATISTICS, McGraw-Hill Book Company, Inc., New York, 1960, pp. 273-358.
45. Nie, Norman, Dale H. Bent, and C. Hadlai Hull, SPSS: STATISTICAL PACKAGE FOR THE SOCIAL SCIENCES, McGraw-Hill Book Company, Inc., New York, 1970, Chapter 17.
46. Hunt, Jr., Isaac C., and Bernard Cohen, MINORITY RECRUITING IN THE NEW YORK CITY POLICE DEPARTMENT. PART I. THE ATTRACTION OF CANDIDATES. PART II. THE RETENTION OF CANDIDATES, R-702-NYC, The New York City-Rand Institute, May 1971.

About the Authors

Dr. Bernard Cohen is an Associate Professor in Sociology at Queens College, City University of New York, and also the Director of the Police Personnel Program at the New York City-Rand Institute. He received his B.A. degree and Master's degree in Hebrew Literature from Yeshiva College in 1959 and 1961, respectively, and an A.M. and Ph.D. degree in Sociology from the University of Pennsylvania in 1964 and 1968, respectively.

At the New York City-Rand Institute, Dr. Cohen recently completed two research projects, one on minority recruitment, and the other on the internal system of police justice in New York City. The findings and recommendations of both studies have been implemented by the New York City Police Department.

Dr. Cohen is the criminology book review editor (1969-) for THE JOURNAL OF CRIMINAL LAW AND CRIMINOLOGY, published for Northwestern University School of Law, and is a past Research Consultant in Criminology for the Department of Health, Education and Welfare, Washington, D.C. Also, Dr. Cohen recently co-authored a book entitled CRIME AND RACE, and he has written many articles on crime and juvenile delinquency.

Dr. Jan M. Chaiken is project director for a New York City-Rand Institute study of the deployment of municipal emergency services sponsored by the U.S. Department of Housing and Urban Development, and he is an Adjunct Associate Professor in the System Science Department of the University of California at Los Angeles. He received his B.S. degree in physics from Carnegie-Mellon University in 1960, and his Ph.D. degree in mathematics from the Massachusetts Institute of Technology in 1966.

Prior to joining the staff of the New York City-Rand Institute in 1968, Dr. Chaiken was an Assistant Professor of Mathematics at Cornell University and a Research Associate at M.I.T., where he was engaged in analysis related to problems of mathematical physics.

At the Institute, Dr. Chaiken was formerly project director for police studies and a member of the group conducting research for the New York City Fire Department. In addition to this work on the relationships of the background characteristics of policemen to their later performance on the job, Dr. Chaiken has conducted studies on prediction of the rates at which emergency calls will be received by fire and police departments, analysis of police manning levels, design of response areas for emergency units, and effectiveness of police activities.

His publications have appeared in OPERATIONS RESEARCH, the JOURNAL OF APPLIED PROBABILITY, and MANAGEMENT SCIENCE. He is the author of a chapter in TECHNIQUES OF OPTIMIZATION, A.V. Balakrishnan (ed.), Academic Press, 1972, and is co-author of a chapter in ANALYSIS OF PUBLIC SYSTEMS, Drake, Keeney, and Morse (eds.), M.I.T. Press, 1972.

Rand Books

Selected Rand Books

Bagdikian, Ben. THE INFORMATION MACHINES: THEIR IMPACT ON MEN AND THE MEDIA. New York: Harper and Row, 1971.

Coleman, James S. and Nancy L. Karweit. INFORMATION SYSTEMS AND PERFORMANCE MEASURES IN SCHOOLS. Englewood Cliffs, N.J.: Educational Technology Publications, 1972.

Dalkey, Norman C. (ed.) STUDIES IN THE QUALITY OF LIFE: DELPHI AND DECISION-MAKING. Lexington, Mass.: D.C. Heath and Company, 1972.

Fisher, Gene H. COST CONSIDERATIONS IN SYSTEMS ANALYSIS. New York: American Elsevier Publishing Company, 1971.

Levien, Roger E. (ed.) THE EMERGING TECHNOLOGY: INSTRUCTIONAL USES OF THE COMPUTER IN HIGHER EDUCATION. New York: McGraw-Hill Book Company, 1972.

Pascal, Anthony H. (ed.) RACIAL DISCRIMINATION IN ECONOMIC LIFE. Lexington, Mass.: D.C. Heath and Company, Inc., 1972.

Pascal, Anthony, H. (ed.) THINKING ABOUT CITIES: NEW PERSPECTIVES ON URBAN PROBLEMS. Belmont, California: Dickenson Publishing Company, 1970.

Newhouse, Joseph P. and Arthur J. Alexander. AN ECONOMICS ANALYSIS OF PUBLIC LIBRARY SERVICES. Lexington, Mass.: D.C. Heath and Company, 1972.

Selected New York City-Rand Institute Publications

Police

APPLYING THE CONCEPTS OF PROGRAM BUDGETING TO THE NEW YORK CITY POLICE DEPARTMENT, A.J. Tenzer, J.B. Benton, C. Teng, RM-5846-NYC, June 1969.

PUBLIC ORDER STUDIES IN NEW YORK CITY, S. Wildhorn, P-4250, November 1969.

AN ANALYSIS OF THE APPREHENSION ACTIVITIES OF THE NEW YORK CITY POLICE DEPARTMENT, P.W. Greenwood, R-529-NYC, September 1970.

THE POLICE INTERNAL ADMINISTRATION OF JUSTICE IN NEW YORK CITY, B. Cohen, R-621-NYC, November 1970.

AIDS TO DECISIONMAKING IN POLICE PATROL, J.S. Kakalik, S. Wildhorn, R-593/4-HUD/RC, February 1971.

MINORITY RECRUITING IN THE NEW YORK CITY POLICE DEPART-
MENT, PART I: THE ATTRACTION OF CANDIDATES; PART II: THE
RETENTION OF CANDIDATES, B. Cohen, I.C. Hunt, Jr., R-702-NYC, May
1971.

IMPROVING PUBLIC SAFETY IN URBAN APARTMENT DWELLINGS:
SECURITY CONCEPTS AND EXPERIMENTAL DESIGN FOR NEW YORK
CITY HOUSING AUTHORITY BUILDINGS, W. Fairley, M.I. Liechenstein,
A.F. Westin, R-655-NYC, June 1971.

MEASURING THE RESPONSE PATTERNS OF NEW YORK CITY POLICE
PATROL CARS, R.C. Larson,* R-673-NYC/HUD, July 1971.

SOME EFFECTS OF AN INCREASE IN POLICE MANPOWER IN THE 20TH
PRECINCT OF NEW YORK CITY, S. James Press, R-704-NYC, October
1971.

Emergency Services

ON INSENSITIVITIES IN URBAN REDISTRICTING AND FACILITY LOCA-
TION, R.C. Larson, K.A. Stevenson, R-533-NYC/HUD, March 1971.

RESPONSE OF EMERGENCY UNITS: THE EFFECTS OF BARRIERS, DIS-
CRETE STREETS, AND ONE-WAY STREETS, R.C. Larson,* R-675-HUD,
April 1971.

METHODS FOR ALLOCATING URBAN EMERGENCY UNITS, J. Chaiken,
R.C. Larson, R-680-HUD/NSF, May 1971.

LINEAR PROGRAMMING MODELS OF CREW ASSIGNMENTS FOR
REFUSE COLLECTION, E. Ignall, P. Kolesar, W. Walker, P-4717, November
1971.

ALLOCATION OF EMERGENCY UNITS: RESPONSE AREAS, J. Chaiken,
P-4745, December 1971.

Other Criminal Justice

THE FLOW OF DEFENDANTS THROUGH THE NEW YORK CITY CRIMI-
NAL COURT IN 1967, J.B. Jennings, RM-6364-NYC, September 1970.

THE FLOW OF ARRESTED ADULT DEFENDANTS THROUGH THE MAN-
HATTAN CRIMINAL COURT IN 1968 AND 1969, J.B. Jennings,
R-638-NYC, January 1971.

POTENTIAL USES OF THE COMPUTER IN CRIMINAL COURTS, P.W.
Greenwood, P-4581, February 1971.

---

*These reports, together with other work conducted at The New York City-Rand Institute,
are included in URBAN POLICE PATROL ANALYSIS, R.C. Larson, Cambridge: The MIT
Press, 1972.

QUANTITATIVE MODELS OF CRIMINAL COURTS, J.B. Jennings, P-4641, May 1971.

EVALUATION OF THE MANHATTAN CRIMINAL COURT'S MASTER CALENDAR PROJECT: PHASE 1, J.B. Jennings, R-1013-NYC, January 1972.

EMPLOYMENT PROBLEMS OF THE EX-OFFENDERS: TESTIMONY BEFORE THE CITY OF NEW YORK COMMISSION ON HUMAN RIGHTS, M. Liechenstein, P-4842. May 1972.

Fire Protection

THE SERVICE FACILITIES OF THE BUREAU OF FIRE COMMUNICATIONS: A COST ANALYSIS OF A PROPOSED CONSOLIDATION, G.S. Levenson, A.J. Tenzer, RM-5726-NYC, September 1968.

FIRE SERVICE: CHALLENGE TO MODERN MANAGEMENT, E.H. Blum, P-4512, November 1970.

A SIMULATION MODEL OF FIRE DEPARTMENT OPERATIONS: DESIGN AND PRELIMINARY RESULTS, G.M. Carter, E. Ignall, R-632-NYC, December 1970.

URBAN FIRE PROTECTION: STUDIES OF THE OPERATIONS OF THE NEW YORK CITY FIRE DEPARTMENT, E.H. Blum, R-681, January 1971.

FIRE INSURANCE AND THE INNER CITY, H.D. Shapiro, R-703-NSF, February 1971.

NUMBER OF EMERGENCY UNITS BUSY AT ALARMS WHICH REQUIRE MULTIPLE SERVERS, J. Chaiken, R-531-NYC/HUD, March 1971.

RESPONSE AREAS FOR TWO EMERGENCY UNITS, G.M. Carter, J. Chaiken, E. Ignall, R-532-NYC/HUD, March 1971.

AN EXTENSION OF ERLANG'S FORMULAS WHICH DISTINGUISHES INDIVIDUAL SERVERS, J. Chaiken, E. Ignall, R-567-NYC/HUD, March 1971.

PREDICTING THE DEMAND FOR FIRE SERVICE, J. Chaiken, J.E. Rolph, P-4625, May 1971.

APPLICATIONS OF SYSTEMS ANALYSIS TO URBAN FIRE PROTECTION, A.J. Swersey, P-4741, November 1971.

AN EARLY DETECTION AND WARNING SYSTEM FOR FIRES IN BUILDINGS, R.D. Doctor, G.S. Levenson, A.J. Tenzer, R-880-NYC, December 1971.

VIRTUAL MEASURES FOR COMPUTER SIMULATION EXPERIMENTS, G.M. Carter, E. Ignall, P-4817, April 1972.

DEPLOYMENT RESEARCH OF THE NEW YORK CITY FIRE PROJECT, E.H. Blum, R-968, May 1972.

TECHNOLOGY AIDS FIRE SERVICE, J.T. O'Hagan, E.H. Blum, P-4872, June 1972.

Health

THE NEW YORK CITY HEALTH BUDGET IN PROGRAM TERMS, C. Teng, RM-5774-NYC, February 1969.

PLANNING PUBLIC EXPENDITURES ON MENTAL HEALTH SERVICE DELIVERY, F.A. Sloan, RM-6339-NYC, February 1971.

THE SUPPLY OF PROFESSIONAL NURSES AND THEIR RECRUITMENT AND RETENTION BY HOSPITALS, K.A. Archibald, R-836-NYC, July 1971.

COST/OUTPUT ANALYSIS OF ALTERNATIVE PROCEDURES FOR A HOSPITAL SURVEILLANCE PROGRAM, R. Goldstein, R-789-NYC, August 1971.

Housing

A GUIDE TO GOVERNMENT ACTIVITIES IN NEW YORK CITY'S HOUSING MARKETS, D.J. Dreyfuss, J. Hendrickson, RM-5673-NYC, November 1968.

RESEARCH ON NEW YORK CITY'S HOUSING PROBLEMS, I.S. Lowry, P-4002, December 1968.

AN ANALYSIS OF ALTERNATIVE MEASURES OF TENANT BENEFITS OF GOVERNMENT HOUSING PROGRAMS WITH ILLUSTRATIVE CALCULATIONS FROM PUBLIC HOUSING, E.O. Olsen, J.R. Prescott, P-4129, November 1969.

CAN PUBLIC CONSTRUCTION AND REHABILITATION INCREASE THE QUANTITY OF HOUSING SERVICE CONSUMED BY LOW-INCOME FAMILIES?, E.O. Olsen, P-4256, December 1969.

THE EFFECTS OF A SIMPLE RENT CONTROL SCHEME IN A COMPETITIVE HOUSING MARKET, E.O. Olsen, P-4257, December 1969.

AN EFFICIENT METHOD OF IMPROVING THE HOUSING OF LOW-INCOME FAMILIES, E.O. Olsen, P-4258, December 1969.

RENTAL HOUSING IN NEW YORK CITY, VOL. I: CONFRONTING THE CRISIS, I.S. Lowry (Ed.), RM-6190-NYC, February 1970.

A METHODOLOGY FOR EVALUATING HOUSING PROGRAMS, J.S. DeSalvo, P-4364, April 1970.

EFFECTS OF THE PROPERTY TAX ON OPERATING AND INVESTMENT DECISIONS OF RENTAL PROPERTY OWNERS, J.S. DeSalvo, P-4437, August 1970.

THE LANDLORD REINVESTMENT MODEL: A COMPUTER-BASED METHOD OF EVALUATING THE FINANCIAL FEASIBILITY OF ALTERNATIVE TREATMENTS FOR PROBLEM BUILDINGS, C.P. Rydell, P-4477, October 1970.

REFORMING RENT CONTROL IN NEW YORK CITY: THE ROLE OF RESEARCH IN POLICY MAKING, I.S. Lowry, P-4570, November 1970.

FACTORS AFFECTING MAINTENANCE AND OPERATING COSTS IN FEDERAL PUBLIC HOUSING PROJECTS, C.P. Rydell, R-634-NYC, December 1970.

HOUSING CODE ENFORCEMENT IN NEW YORK CITY, M.B. Teitz, S.R. Rosenthal, R-648-NYC, April 1971.

HOUSING ASSISTANCE FOR LOW-INCOME URBAN FAMILIES: A FRESH APPROACH, I.S. Lowry, P-4645, May 1971.

RENTAL HOUSING IN NEW YORK CITY. VOL. II: THE DEMAND FOR SHELTER, I.S. Lowry, J.S. DeSalvo, B.M. Woodfill, R-649-NYC, June 1971.

FACTORS AFFECTING MAINTENANCE AND OPERATING COSTS IN PRIVATE RENTAL HOUSING, K.M. Eisenstadt, R-1055-NYC, August 1972.

WELFARE HOUSING IN NEW YORK CITY, I.S. Lowry, J.M. Guéron, and K.M. Eisenstadt, R-1164-NYC, November 1972.

Economic Development

INCOME GUARANTEES AND THE WORKING POOR IN NEW YORK CITY: THE EFFECT OF INCOME MAINTENANCE PROGRAMS ON THE HOURS OF WORK OF MALE FAMILY HEADS, D.H. Greenberg, R-658-NYC, March 1971.

EMPLOYMENT IN THE NEW YORK METROPOLITAN AREA, W.A. Johnson, R-571-NYC, December 1971.

Water Pollution

A WATER-QUALITY SIMULATION MODEL FOR WELL MIXED ESTUARIES AND COASTAL SEAS, VOLUME I: PRINCIPLES OF COMPUTATION, J.J. Leendertse, RM-6230-RC, February 1970.

A WATER-QUALITY SIMULATION MODEL FOR WELL MIXED ESTUARIES AND COASTAL SEAS, VOL. II: COMPUTATION PROCEDURES, J.J. Leendertse, E.C. Gritton, R-708-NYC, July 1971.

A WATER-QUALITY SIMULATION MODEL FOR WELL MIXED ESTUARIES AND COASTAL SEAS, VOL. III: JAMAICA BAY SIMULATION, J.J. Leendertse, E.C. Gritton, R-709-NYC, July 1971.

A WATER-QUALITY SIMULATION MODEL FOR WELL MIXED ESTUARIES AND COASTAL SEAS, VOL. IV: JAMAICA BAY TIDAL FLOWS, J.J. Leendertse, R-1009-NYC, July 1972.

A WATER-QUALITY SIMULATION MODEL FOR WELL MIXED ESTUARIES AND COASTAL SEAS, VOL. V: JAMAICA BAY RAINSTORMS, E.C. Gritton, R-1010-NYC, July 1972.

Neighborhood Studies

SOCIAL REPORTING FOR A CITY: A PERSPECTIVE AND SOME PROB-
LEMS, M.H. Krieger, P-4651, May 1971.
NEIGHBORHOOD GOVERNMENT, D. Yates, P-4671, July 1971.
THE CONTEMPORARY CITY AND CONTEMPORARY SOCIAL RESEARCH,
R.K. Yin, P-4680, July 1971.
PARTICIPANT-OBSERVATION AND THE DEVELOPMENT OF URBAN
NEIGHBORHOOD POLICY, R.K. Yin, R-962, May 1972.
POLICY USES OF URBAN INDICATORS, R.K. Yin, P-4829, May 1972.
SOME REMARKS ON EVALUATING ADMINISTRATIVE DECENTRALI-
ZATION, R.K. Yin, P-4844, June 1972.
POPULATION AND HOUSING IN EAST HARLEM, 1950-1970, J. Goering, M.
Robison, J. Gonzalez, R.K. Yin, P-4854, June 1972.

City Government

INTRODUCING TECHNOLOGICAL CHANGE IN A BUREAUCRATIC
STRUCTURE, R.W. Archibald, R.B. Hoffman, P-4025, February 1969.
WORKING WITH A CITY GOVERNMENT: RAND'S EXPERIENCE IN NEW
YORK, P.L. Szanton, RM-6236, January 1970.
CITIES OF THE MIND, D. Yates, P-4754, January 1972.
ANALYSIS AND URBAN GOVERNMENT: EXPERIENCE OF THE NEW
YORK CITY–RAND INSTITUTE, P.L. Szanton, P-4822, April 1972.

Index

Absence from post without permission, 43

Absenteeism, rate of, 7, 9, 46-47, 49, 51, 54, 65, 69, 74, 85, 90, 94, 100, 105, 116, 125

Accidents: automobile, 32; subject to, 7, 14; victims of, 1

Active/inactive status, 32

Administrative functions and positions, 1, 4, 12, 40, 122

Age: and absenteeism, 54; at appointment, 4-6, 22-23; and career type, 52; and civilian complaints, 54; and disciplinary actions, 52; influence of, 22, 38-40, 49, 53, 85, 101-110, 117-118, 128; and intelligence, 66; and performance, 51-54

Alcoholism, 44, 77

Amendments, constitutional, 79

Appointment: age at, 4-6; of black officers, 50; criteria for, 3, 9; detective, 120; educational level, 31, 59; municipal, 127; as patrolman, 23; prerequisite, 3, 9

Aptitude, 5-6

Arrests, 49-50; false, 43, 73, 76, 119; felony, 21, 48-49; history of, 30, 32, 38-40, 49, 73-74, 103, 107, 117-118; misdemeanor, 21, 48-49; number of, 42, 48; and rights of persons, 73; prior, 74, 119. *See also* Crimes

Aspirations, low, 5

Assignments: first, 36: history of, 21; procedures, 4, 19; special, 40

Attitudes and orientation, 14, 48

Authority, abuse of, 21, 44, 52, 54, 58, 71-72, 78, 97

Awards, and current residence, 99; departmental, 9, 21, 41-42, 119; and I.Q., 55, 57, 59; number of, 42, 120; and performance, 76; and recruit scores, 90-91; receipt of, 41-42, 49, 51, 54, 61, 67, 69, 73, 82-83, 87, 93, 96, 102-103, 111-112, 115-116, 125

BFF study, 8-9

Background: characteristics, 3-5, 48,

50, 96; data, 10, 13; elements, 9, 16, 20-21; factors, 21, 101-102, 105-107, 126; investigators, 6, 20, 22, 26, 28, 32-33, 37, 77, 82-83, 85-86, 123-124, 127; rating, 33, 38-40, 67, 77, 82, 84, 101, 105, 107, 110, 118-119; variables, 33, 37, 51, 114-115, 126

Baehr, Melany E., cited, 5-6, 8

Baltimore City Police Department, 15

Behavior, dimensions of, 20, 43, 125

Birth, region of, 24-25, 49-50, 65-66, 101-107, 119, 125

Black officers: appointments and promotions, 50, 82; actives, 37, 72, 110-111, 118; career type, 87; complaints, 43-46; and debts, 29-30; detectives, 50; disqualifications, 79; education, 36, 59; 124; harassment complaints, 43, 67; I.Q., 55, 57, 105-106, 119; general, 1-2, 16, 20, 22, 36, 74, 80, 98, 114, 121-122, 125-126; performance ratings, 9; and black population, 36; recruit scores, 105-106; region of birth, 25, 65-66; Socio-Economic Index, 25-26; sub-cohort, 20, 37-42, 51, 54-55, 73, 76-77, 85, 87, 90, 93-94, 115; times sick, 94

Blum, Richard E., 5-6, 12-14

Brutality, accusations of, 21, 44

Burglaries, 44

California Psychological Inventory, 15

Captain, rank of, 15, 28, 55, 57, 61, 80-83, 87, 95, 109, 120

Career: advancement, 17, 40-41, 64, 66, 69, 83, 112, 116, 120-121, 124, 128; development, 7; profiles, 120; type, 40-41, 51-57, 60-63, 67, 69, 83, 87-88, 95, 102-104, 108, 111, 115-118, 125

Chaiken, Jan M., cited, 6

Chance vs *Board of Education of the City of New York*, 79

Character and characteristics, personal, 1, 15-16, 21, 37, 77

Charges: departmental, 19, 21, 43, 49-52, 61, 64, 67, 71, 85, 89,